the

man

in

the

green

shirt

miles

davis

the

man

in

the

green

shirt

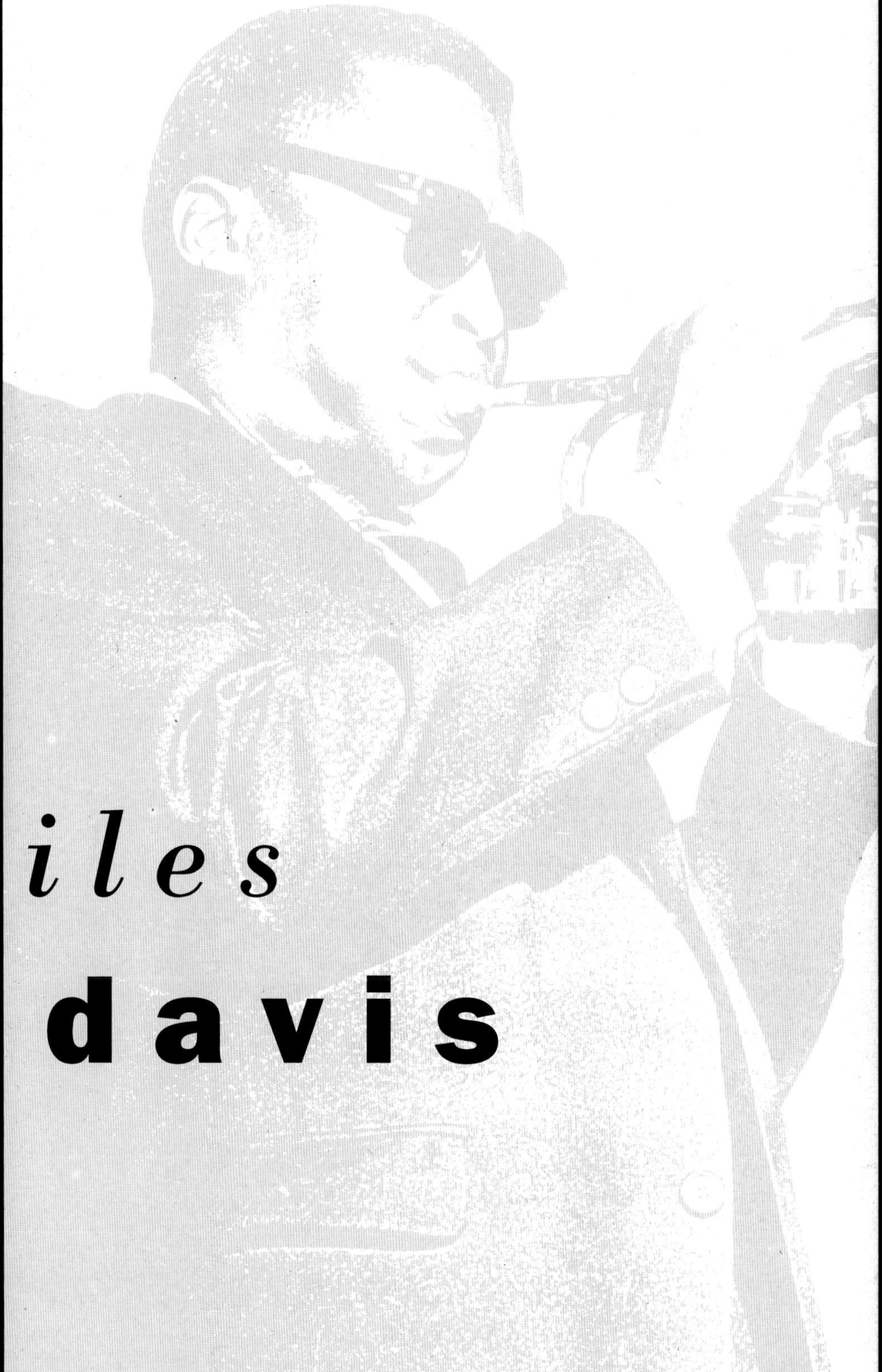

richard

williams

*m*iles

davis

HENRY HOLT AND COMPANY
NEW YORK

Henry Holt and Company, Inc.
Publishers since 1866
115 West 18th Street
New York, New York 10011

Henry Holt ® is a registered trademark of Henry Holt
and Company, Inc.

First published in the United States in 1993 by
Henry Holt and Company, Inc.
Originally published in Great Britain in 1993 by
Bloomsbury Publishing Ltd.

PICTURE SOURCES

George Avakian: 59, 70
USA Today/Contact/Robert Deutsch/Colorific!: 163
Frank Driggs Collection: 13, 21, 23, 26-7, 29, 30-1, 44,
50-1, 73, 74
Popsie Randolph/Frank Driggo Collection: 35, 36-7, 41,
56
Jean-Pierre Leloir: 71
Herman Leonard: 38-9, 42-3, 55, 57, 83, 153, 172-3,
179, 186
Guy le Querrec/Magnum: 119, 122, 160
Dennis Stock/Magnum: 9, 67, 75, 76, 78-9
Bengt H. Malmqvist: 60, 63, 65, 91-4, 96-9, 101-2, 104
Jim Marshall: 116-17, 126, 128, 130-4, 136-43, 146
Photo X/Paudras: 12, 33
Jan Persson: 89, 110-13, 144-5, 148-9, 155 *top*, 158,
162, 164-6, 169 *top*, 171, 174 *top*, 175
Giuseppe Pino: 123, 135
David Redfern: 109, 115, 120, 125, 155 *bottom*, 156,
167, 170, 180, 181 *top left*
Max Jones Files/Redferns: 48, 81
Dany Gignoux/Redferns: 181 *bottom*, 182, 184-5
William Gottlieb/Redferns: 20, 24
Mike Hutson/Redferns: 178
Bob Willoughby/Redferns: 45
Don Hunstein/Sony: 66, 105, 189
Alan Titmuss: 161, 168, 169 *bottom*, 176, 183, 187
J.P. Carbonnier/Top: 47
Val Wilmer: 88, 102 *bottom*, 103, 114, 129

Library of Congress Catalog Card Number: 93-79501

ISBN 0-8050-2704-1

Henry Holt books are available for special promotions
and premiums.
For details contact: Director, Special Markets.

First American Edition—1993

Designed by Bradbury and Williams

Picture research by Anne-Marie Ehrlich

Printed in Italy
All first editions are printed on acid-free paper. ∝

10 9 8 7 6 5 4 3 2 1

For Jack and Laura

'*If you understood everything I said, you'd be me*'

MILES DAVIS

contents

a man
to watch

it was the green shirt. Charlie Parker had the headlong genius, Thelonious Monk had the beatnik weirdness and Charlie Mingus had the rebel soul. But only Miles Davis had the green shirt. There it was, on the cover of *Milestones*, one of the handful of late-fifties albums that turned him from a gifted bebop musician into a figure of godlike remoteness and potency. Inside that cover was music such as had never been heard before: a kind of jazz at once full-blooded and exquisitely refined, meticulously planned yet bursting with magical improvisation, displaying an aristocratic restraint while utterly unafraid of its mission to reveal the future.

That shirt, the green shirt with the perfect button-down collar, was as good an emblem as any of Miles Davis's inextinguishable need to be the coolest man on the planet. But it symbolised more than just an aesthetic: it spoke of an entire set of values.

It may also have been jazz's first serious piece of image-manipulation, and in a way that is as important a statement about Miles Davis as anything in his music. In the late fifties, jazz albums were usually decorated with pictures of scantily clad girls (generally white, generally blonde) or rather self-consciously crude pen-and-ink drawings of the Musician as Noble Savage. In the photograph on the cover of *Milestones* – taken at the behest of Davis's record company by Dennis Stock, the Magnum photographer who had produced some of the most effective icon-building images of James Dean – the trumpeter sits on an elegantly plain fifties-moderne chair; his right hand lies on the thigh of his dark slacks, his left hand supports the trumpet, whose bell rests lightly on the plain curved disc of the seat. He looks at the camera with a calm, level gaze. His face is strong and beautiful, like Muhammad Ali's before things went fuzzy. And the shirt tells you almost as much as the music inside.

That it spoke to a large number of people who wished to identify and share those values became clear when Miles Davis died, in September 1991, aged 65. The deaths of Louis Armstrong, Duke Ellington, Charlie Parker and John Coltrane had all been mourned; but

Davis's departure brought forth a deeper emotion, for his being had represented something beyond music. Of course, the effect on the music was important enough: for a moment, the creative momentum of the century's most vital musical language suddenly seemed to be stalled by the silencing of one man. Jazz people, the hard core and the distant fringe alike, had followed him from Ivy League jackets to silks and velvets, from the suave sophistication of 'My Funny Valentine' to the wild funk of his electronic bands. They had grown so used to relying on his sense of direction that they didn't know where to turn.

To say that he had a magnetic presence would be to understate his effect on any room he entered. One winter night in 1970 I watched him leaning against the bar in a short-lived New York club called Ungano's, listening to Lifetime, the band led by his protégé, the drummer Tony Williams. Davis was wearing a suit made of chamois leather patches; his silver Lamborghini Miura was parked on the kerb, right under a Tow-away Zone sign. The four members of Lifetime were playing like a hurricane, filling the room with howling noise. Everybody was listening, but no one was watching. No one, anyway, apart from the man in the chamois leather suit leaning on the bar. The rest of us were watching him.

Right up to the end, he was a hypnotically attractive figure. Louis Armstrong was jazz's first great soloist, Duke Ellington became its most eminent composer, Charlie Parker burned with the fiercest brilliance, and John Coltrane revealed an entire level of spiritual inquiry. But Miles Davis was somehow more than this. He was beyond idiom, beyond category. Like Ali and Picasso, he was much larger than his chosen medium. More than any other jazzman, he made music that had an existence beyond the dimensions of melody, harmony and rhythm. The totality of Miles Davis was the embodiment of an entire scope of feeling, a complete new kit of attitudes. Above all he was the symbol of jazz as the hipster's music, creating the image of the elegant outsider whose sole concern was to keep the straight world at a distance. In the late fifties one read *L'étranger* and *On the Road*, looked at James Dean and Juliette Gréco, and listened to Miles Davis. In the strange, shifting post-war years, loss and alienation suddenly seemed deeply attractive, dangerous but infinitely desirable gifts to those seeking an oblique response to the Western world's drive towards security and prosperity.

Miles Davis loved risk, and continued to do so all the way through a career in which change was virtually the only constant. This itself was dangerous in a world as paranoid and fissiparous as the little community of jazz people, with its full complement of ticket-inspectors and thought-police. Quite early on, some people came to the conclusion that it was all a contrivance, that such self-consciousness could not be trusted. In fact it was integral to his character, and therefore to his work. Without its promptings, there could have been no *Milestones*; Davis would have been content to play out his life as a Charlie Parker disciple. The imperatives behind the music and the green shirt were identical and indivisible; in fact it was the same imperative, and it was what drove him to rewrite jazz's book of rules three or four times in his life, thereby affecting countless musicians around the world.

Every time he changed, of course, some horrified fans fell away. That was part of the risk, and he never wavered. The biggest falling away came when he embraced rock music at the end of the sixties. Eventually it became clear that he was never going to wear a mohair suit and a polka-dot tie and play 'My Funny Valentine' again. You may not have liked his re-engagement with black street styles, either musical (funk-based) or sartorial (a rather dodgy collection of duster coats, boleros and harem pants in a variety of diaphanous boudoir fabrics); in fact you may very well have hated it. You may not have liked the feverish, morbid noise made by the guitar-based bands he led in the early seventies. You may have watched in horror in the eighties as he encouraged his young sidemen – hardly, as individuals, on the level of the talent he had uncovered in previous decades – to turn up their amps to the max and whack out clichés by the yard. But you had to accept that this was a sensibility that couldn't stand to be

anywhere other than at the front; the fact that his front might not have been the same as yours was neither here nor there.

Despite a life that many people would regard as the last word in self-indulgence, Miles Davis had a rigorous and unsparing approach to his art. He demanded a lot of himself (imagine how easy and lucrative it would have been for him to coast through the last 30 years of his life playing 'Autumn Leaves' and 'Love for Sale'), and he demanded a lot of his listeners. He never opted for the entertainer's tactic of pleasing you with something you already knew: he didn't even believe in giving you clues as to what the unfamiliar thing he was doing might be. He turned his back on the audience or left the stage because he thought they should have better things to do than stare at him when he wasn't playing.

Someone like that can make us think about the fundamental principles of art, about what it is for and what it can do, and what it can tell us about ourselves, as well as about the artist who made it. Without the green shirt, an awful lot of modern music would have been very different. A lot of post-war lives, too.

1

boy with

a horn

*b*oy *with* **a horn**

Previous pages:

Left: The young Miles Dewey Davis III in the mid-thirties.

Right: Miles Davis's first professional job was with Earl Randle's orchestra at the Club Rhumboogie in St Louis. Here they are in 1944, with Davis at the extreme right of the trumpet section.

from day one, Miles Davis knew what beauty was. Any time he wanted, all he had to do was look at his mother's face: at her neat features, big brown eyes and strong mouth, its upper lip arching into an expression at once pouting and sardonic. And when Cleota Henry married Miles Dewey Davis II, there were beauty and brains on both sides.

Both parents came from Arkansas, where they were children of the black middle class. Miles Dewey Davis I was a hard-working book-keeper who used his money to buy 500 acres of farmland and was able to send his sons to university. Miles II had graduated from Arkansas Baptist College, Lincoln University and Northwestern University's College of Dentistry when he married Cleota and took her north to Alton, Illinois, on the Mississippi River. Their first child, a daughter, whom they named Dorothy, was born in 1924. The second, a son, came along two years later, on 26 May 1926 – a pretty baby, with his mother's features. They extended the family tradition and called him Miles Dewey Davis III. The following year the family moved a few miles south, to the cattle town of East St Louis, where Miles II set up his dental practice; they established their home in an apartment above a drugstore on 15th Street. A year later, a second son, Vernon, was born.

Miles II had inherited his father's strong character, demanding nature and concern for personal prosperity. He liked nice cars and good clothes, but he was also politically aware, with a strong interest in justice and, specifically, the rights of black people. An admirer of the back-to-Africa theories of Marcus Garvey and a stern opponent of compromise, he imbued his children with a powerful belief in their own equality and with an understanding that accepting second-best would get them nowhere. 'If I got my sense of style and clothes from my mother,' Miles III would later say, 'I think I got most of my attitude, my sense of who I was, my confidence and race pride, from my father.' Both parents, though, seem to have had formidable personalities, and from his mother the young Miles also acquired the love of music that was to bring him to the world's notice. The glamorous, mink-clad Cleo Davis played the piano and the violin; back in Arkansas, her own mother had been an organ teacher. On the Davis side, there had been a tradition of playing classical music for the plantation owners.

The clever and stylish Davises were a discordant couple, though, and their temperamental differences would eventually lead them to divorce. Nevertheless, during the early years of their marriage they became people of significance in East St Louis; at one point Miles II even ran, albeit unsuccessfully, for election as State Representative. Yet their offspring, like the other black children from their neighbourhood, had no choice but to attend the segregated John Robinson School, where good teachers – including two granddaughters of Nat Turner, the slave leader – struggled with poor facilities. As they walked to school every morning, Dorothy and Miles III passed the far better endowed establishment for white children. The contrast could hardly fail to stick in their minds; their father's inspiration had already led them to see such obvious inequality as something not to be accepted and made the best of, but to be resented and resisted.

The boy Miles's first interest was sport. He wasn't big or strong, but he ran, swam, rode (on regular visits to his grandfather's farm in Arkansas) and played football and baseball. Most significantly, he boxed, and embarked on a lifelong study and admiration of the great black fighters, from Jack Johnson through Joe Louis to Muhammad Ali.

Music was in the house from the beginning. The three children put on their own little shows, and at the age of nine or ten Miles III received his first trumpet, as a present from his father's best friend, Dr John Eubanks, their next-door neighbour. Listening to the radio, mostly to a show called 'Harlem Rhythms', he began to register the popular big bands of the time: those led by Duke Ellington, Fletcher Henderson, Jimmie Lunceford, Count Basie. And, of course, the trumpeters: Louis Armstrong, with his own band and that of Lionel Hampton; Ellington's Bubber Miley, Cootie Williams and Rex Stewart; Basie's Hot Lips Page and Buck Clayton; and the talented white performers, like the virtuoso Harry James and the lyrical Bobby Hackett. On those visits to Arkansas, too, he heard the sounds of country blues and gospel music; later, for all Miles Davis's urbane sophistication, there would be at the very core of his music a profound understanding of the blues.

At Boy Scout camp, he was invited to perform Taps and Reveille: a memorable and significant event in a young boy's life, being perhaps the first recognition outside his family of a developing individual skill. Now a pupil at Crispus Attucks Junior High, he was taking lessons from another friend of his father, Elwood Buchanan, who was a teacher at Lincoln High School. When Davis himself moved up to Lincoln High, he absorbed even more of the influence of Buchanan, whom he was later to describe as 'my first great teacher'. It was Buchanan, in fact, who talked the family into buying young Miles a new horn for his thirteenth birthday, against the desire of his mother, who unavailingly would have preferred her son to play the more genteel violin.

Cleo Davis may have been somewhat mollified by the identity of Miles's new trumpet teacher: the leader of the St Louis Symphony Orchestra's trumpet section, a German named Gustav, who took him further into the realms of 'legitimate' technique and taught him about mouthpieces. But the city was also turning into the breeding ground of another type of trumpet-player, and it was of this type that Miles learnt from Elwood Buchanan.

St Louis's jazz trumpeters weren't the bold, brassy players who had developed their craft in New Orleans street parades and come up the river in the great migration of the twenties and thirties. The 'St Louis sound' was calmer, more reflective, with a stronger emphasis on melodic values. By the time Miles was old enough to tell the difference, its chief exponent was Harold 'Shorty' Baker, who had been with Don Redman, Teddy Wilson and, briefly, Duke Ellington. Elwood Buchanan encouraged Miles to listen to men like Baker, and to develop a round, vibrato-less tone, even when the Lincoln High band was playing a Sousa march. Struck by his pupil's talent and his voracious desire for knowledge,

Buchanan told Miles's father that his son wouldn't be following him into dentistry, but had the makings of a professional musician.

No one, however, had a stronger influence on the teenaged Miles Davis than the young man who was to become the most renowned exponent of the St Louis approach to the trumpet. Five years older than Miles, Clark Terry was an instant role model: already a consummate musician and a man of the world, he was an embryonic hipster with cool clothes, a powerful interest in girls and an eloquent and original trumpet style in which a dry wit took precedence over hot licks. At first, understandably, the older man – a friend of Elwood Buchanan – paid little attention to the schoolboy.

It was with a fellow trumpeter of his own age that Miles joined the American Federation of Musicians – the union of his chosen profession. He and his friend Bobby Danzig were both 15 and spending their nights sneaking into clubs to listen to older musicians when they paid their first subscriptions, which in Danzig's case probably came from the proceeds of his other career, as a gifted pickpocket. Miles was more interested in chromatic scales than petty crime, and was starting to put his own little bands together. With friends including a pianist, Duke Brooks, and a drummer, Nick Haywood, he practised in the basement of the new family house on 17th Street, and played any little engagements he could find, including his first weekend road trips.

At 16, he started going out with the mother of his first three children. Irene Birth, a fellow student at Lincoln High, was a pretty, light-skinned girl whose family lived in a poorer neighbourhood near the railroad and the cattle pens. Two years older than Miles, she was already performing with a dance troupe in East St Louis and encouraged him to go for a job with a popular local band, Earl Randle's Blue Devils. Miles successfully auditioned for a vacancy in the trumpet section and joined the band for its residency across the Mississippi at the Rhumboogie Club in downtown St Louis.

During his year with Randle, Miles learned many aspects of his craft. Some, such as how to accompany singers, dancers and comedians, would be of limited value in the future. Others, like the chore of organising rehearsals, with which Randle entrusted the young apprentice, would provide a good grounding for his own later career as a leader. He also absorbed further lessons in theory from the more experienced members of the band, while life on the road gave him first-hand exposure to other bands playing the Midwestern circuit. Clark Terry came to hear him at the Rhumboogie and the two became firm friends, travelling together to jam sessions in the area; he met Lester Young, Sonny Stitt, Benny Carter and Roy Eldridge. By the time he graduated from Lincoln High, at the beginning of 1944, he was getting offers from other bandleaders to leave Randle and go with them: soon he had the choice of Tiny Bradshaw, Illinois Jacquet or McKinney's Cotton Pickers. None of them, though, could match the $80 a week Randle was paying him.

Davis's solid professional progress was in contrast to the turmoil in his family life. His father was spending more and more time on the 300-acre farm he had bought out of town, and eventually he and Cleota separated. At about the same time, in the summer of 1944, Irene gave birth to a daughter, Cheryl. Not surprisingly, Miles's thoughts were beginning to turn away from East St Louis, and in June he travelled to Chicago with Adam Lambert's Six Brown Cats, a band from New Orleans.

The move was not a success. After a few weeks of growing musical dissatisfaction, he returned home to rethink his future. He had graduated from high school, so dental college was still a possibility, but he also contemplated following Clark Terry into the US Navy, since the Navy Band based at Great Lakes contained many fine jazz musicians and the bandsmen's life was a fairly easy one. Then, though, the Billy Eckstine Orchestra came to St Louis.

That summer, a musical revolution was underway a few hundred miles to the east. In the clubs of New York, on 52nd Street and uptown in Harlem, young musicians tired of the constraints of the big bands which paid their wages were experimenting with the next phase of jazz. In after-hours jam sessions at Minton's Playhouse and Monroe's

Uptown House, the trumpeter Dizzy Gillespie, alto saxophonist Charlie Parker, guitarist Charlie Christian, pianist Thelonious Monk and drummer Kenny Clarke were creating a laboratory for the research and development of a new jazz which was coming to be known by its onomatopoeic nickname: bebop.

In contrast to earlier forms of jazz, bebop was oblique, elliptical, cryptic, at its most satisfying to its participants when it became virtually unintelligible to outsiders. Up to this point, jazz and its related idioms, from jug-band music through ragtime to swing, had been thought of as being strictly for entertainment – even when, as with Armstrong's 'West End Blues', Robert Johnson's 'Love in Vain' or Ellington's 'Mood Indigo', they unquestionably fulfilled the criteria of high art. Coming out of the traditions of vaudeville and the minstrel show, jazz musicians were expected to wear uniforms, to stand up and sit down to order, to create excitement on demand. In the dance halls, the customer was king and the discipline was military. But jazz in the mid-forties was evolving at such a rate that it could no longer be bound by the methods and mores of show business.

Bebop, then, was the hip musician's revenge on the squares: it was angular and unpredictable, as if its whole purpose were to create surprise. It held no comfort, offered no resolution. Its characteristic harmonic interval was the flattened fifth, which exists on the keyboard but to the Western ear is like a

colour that does not appear in nature. From that basis, the harmonies took off into an exotic parallel universe of substitute chords and extensions. Rhythmically it was just as adventurous, keeping the regular 4/4 rhythm but abandoning the emphasis on the backbeat common to all earlier forms of jazz, so enabling drummers to respond to a soloist's line with spontaneous punctuation and decoration. Since much of it was played at blindingly fast speeds, the requirements of dancers were clearly no longer this music's point.

Bebop was complex, fluid, technically advanced. It was also utterly stripped of polite gestures and signs of deference. A generation of young black musicians had watched the new vocabulary of jazz being appropriated and diluted for popular consumption by whites, whose relationship with the entertainment business ensured that they received rewards denied to the music's originators. Armstrong and Ellington were moderately famous; but Harry James and Glenn Miller were rich. Bebop was the black musician saying: okay, sucker, try stealing this.

To earn their living, most of the early bebop musicians still played in the big bands – Gillespie with Teddy Hill and Cab Calloway, Parker with Jay McShann, Noble Sissle and Earl Hines. Disaffected and mutinous, held in check by tightly circumscribed musical arrangements and old standards of presentation, they yearned for a better environment in which to express themselves. In the clubs and jam sessions, small groups were the norm – and the format of a quintet or sextet offered the flexibility and space required for extended improvisation. But still, as the Second World War drew to its close, big bands were what drew the paying customers in large numbers and attracted the favour of the booking agents, so the dream was to create a big band that could somehow play bebop.

Billy Eckstine was a singer and trumpeter with matinée-idol looks and fine musical taste. As the featured male singer with the Earl Hines Orchestra, he had encountered Charlie Parker and the new theories of bebop. In 1944, aged 30, Eckstine could have launched a commercial career; instead, for a brief but incandescent period, he led one of the most extraordinary jazz ensembles of all time. When it reached the Riviera Club in St Louis that summer, the Billy Eckstine Orchestra was packed with raging beboppers: Gillespie and Parker were flanked by the tenor saxophonists Lucky Thompson and Gene Ammons; the fire-breathing Art Blakey was the drummer; Sarah Vaughan – who had been in Hines's band with Eckstine, Parker and Gillespie – was the female singer.

Miles Davis had already heard Gillespie and Parker on record. Parker's first recorded improvisation, on Jay McShann's 1941 'Hootie Blues', had struck young Miles hard: a dozen bars of languid double time and harmonic ingenuity that ignited a medium-tempo Kansas City set piece and provided an enigmatic foreshadowing of the coming explosion. In the spring of 1944 the great tenorist Coleman Hawkins had godfathered the new music by gathering together a bunch of beboppers and recording Dizzy's 'Woody 'n' You', with a solo by the trumpeter. Thus primed, Miles Davis was nevertheless astonished by the impact of the Eckstine band, to the extent that in his last years he was to describe hearing it as the greatest musical feeling of his life. Even better for this wide-eyed 18-year-old was the sensation when he was invited to play with the band.

He had taken his trumpet to the Riviera Club, just in case. And he had hardly set foot in the place when a man came up to him, asked if he could play that thing and if he had a union card, explained that one of the band's trumpeters was sick and invited him to take the missing man's chair. The man issuing the invitation turned out to be Dizzy Gillespie. For the remainder of the two-week engagement Miles Davis sat in the trumpet section, sight-reading the charts and marvelling at the spirit and creativity of Gillespie, Parker and the rest of the young revolutionaries.

'I've come close to matching the feeling of that night in 1944 in music, when I first heard Diz and Bird,' he was to say in his autobiography; 'but I've never quite got there.' And at that moment his mind was made up: he was on his way to New York.

inside

bebop

h e was looking for Diz and Bird. As far as his parents were concerned, he was in New York to study composition at the celebrated Juilliard Conservatory, on 66th Street. For Miles, though, there was only one reason to be in New York: the chance to get next to the founding fathers of bebop, on the morning after its birth.

His father had paid his tuition fees and given him a little spending money, plus an allowance of $40 a week. The Juilliard people found him a place to stay, but he soon moved to lodgings of his own choosing, a rooming house on 147th Street run by a family from East St Louis. The real co-ordinates of Miles Davis's New York City, though, were laid down by 52nd Street, where jazz clubs – the Onyx, the Three Deuces, Kelly's Stable, the Downbeat, the Famous Door and many others – lined the blocks between 5th and 8th Avenues, and 118th Street, where the owner of Minton's Playhouse, the bandleader Teddy Hill, allowed the young generation their heads at his increasingly popular Monday night jam sessions.

While he was looking for his erstwhile

colleagues in the Billy Eckstine band, he found other musicians whose paths he'd crossed back home, notably the brilliant young trumpeters Freddie Webster and Fats Navarro. These two had very different approaches to the horn. Navarro, a 21-year-old from Key West, of mixed African, Cuban and Chinese blood, took Gillespie's pyrotechnics and added a burnished lyricism. Webster, a 27-year-old from Cleveland, had a round, luscious tone, a measured delivery and a fondness for playing ballads. Davis and Webster started hanging out together right away, visiting clubs and working out new ideas. At this stage, Miles shared his new friend's interest in women and the trumpet, but not his addiction to heroin, nor his liking for carrying a gun.

Davis was asking everyone he met – Dexter Gordon, Max Roach, Coleman Hawkins – where he could find his idols. Eventually someone gave him Gillespie's number and he was invited to visit the older man's Harlem apartment. But Dizzy didn't know where Bird was, either, and it was a while before Davis tracked him to an uptown club called the Heatwave. Parker looked in terrible

Previous pages:

Left: The great tenor saxophonist **Coleman Hawkins, a brave patron of the young beboppers, was among Davis's early employers in New York.**

Right: The patterned suit, the satin tie, the processed hair, the golden horn: ready for success in postwar New York.

He went to New York to look for Charlie Parker, and the alto saxophonist became his mentor. The quintet at the Three Deuces on 52nd Street in 1947: (from left) bassist Tommy Potter, Parker, Davis, pianist Duke Jordan. The drummer, obscured by Parker, would have been Max Roach.

shape but played with undisturbed genius and treated the importunate young trumpeter with courtesy and kindness. It wasn't long before he had moved into Davis's apartment on 147th Street, although when Irene Birth unexpectedly turned up just before Christmas, accompanied by Miles's baby daughter, Cheryl, Bird switched to another room in the same house.

In New York, Parker and Gillespie gave him exactly what he'd hoped for: entry into the world of bebop, plus free lessons in the language. Gillespie showed him the new harmonic theories, writing chords on the backs of matchbooks, while just listening to Parker warming up his horn was an inspiration. When Davis showed up on a Monday night at Minton's, Diz and Bird invited him to play, and he soon became friends with

other young musicians, including the trombonist J.J. Johnson, the drummer Max Roach and the eccentric pianist and composer Thelonious Monk, whose fondness for leaving unpredictable silences in his solos intrigued and impressed Davis. So enthralling was all this activity that the conservatory, and its burden of the white classical tradition, was beginning to weigh heavy. 'I could learn more in one session at Minton's,' Davis later said, 'than it would take me two years to learn at Juilliard.' Nevertheless, he took the opportunity to learn piano, to polish his technique on his primary instrument with the aid of advice from the trumpeters of the New York Philharmonic, and to become further acquainted with the language of the European tradition, particularly that of

Howard McGhee (right) also played with Parker, but his stylistic preference was for the Gillespie approach.

the more modern composers, including Prokofiev and Berg.

Davis was now a regular at jam sessions around town, and was beginning to sit in with established groups. Coleman Hawkins, the first great jazz tenor saxophonist and a man with the unusual habit of giving the next generation a helping hand, welcomed the young trumpeter, a gesture which gave Davis the chance to play alongside the Hawkins band's singer, Billie Holiday. His first formal New York nightclub job came early in 1945, with the band of another big-toned tenorist, 24-year-old Eddie 'Lockjaw' Davis, at the Spotlite on 52nd Street. That May, too, Miles entered a recording studio for the first time. As a member of a scratch quintet led by the tenorist and clarinettist Herbie Fields, he accompanied the singer Rubberlegs Williams on four songs for the New Jersey-based Savoy label. Best described as 'novelty blues', they mixed nonsense and ribaldry in a cheerful but fairly nondescript way, allowing a little space for the trumpeter to weave tentative obligatos around the singer.

The first really significant step in Davis's professional career came in the autumn of 1945, when Gillespie broke up his partnership with Parker, and Bird invited Davis to take his place. Pausing only to quit his courses at Juilliard and transfer his union membership from the St Louis branch to New York's Local 802, the 19-year-old Davis opened as a fully fledged member of Parker's quintet at the Three Deuces in October, with Al Haig on piano, Curley Russell on bass and Max Roach on drums.

Right away, it was obvious that the new man didn't sound like Gillespie, even though he might briefly have hoped to. His playing wasn't as fast, and it didn't stretch as phenomenally high; he didn't attempt to emulate his predecessor's explosive power or his swashbuckling insouciance. He was technically gifted, and by now a schooled musician, but his solos had a more diffident air, imposing themselves more by stealth than by brute force. Davis later concluded that, after Gillespie, Parker had wanted a change, and that's undoubtedly what he got.

Before the end of the year the quintet was in the studio for the first time, recording for Savoy. Strangely, Gillespie was back – but to play piano on four of the six tunes, deputising for the designated pianist, Bud Powell, the newest member of the quintet, who had replaced Al Haig but was absent,

apparently on a family visit. Parker had also called up a third pianist, Argonne Thornton, who took over from Gillespie on two tunes. This session turned out two classics: 'Now's the Time', Parker's funkiest blues, with a simple theme also in circulation under the title 'The Hucklebuck'; and 'Ko-Ko', an up-tempo variation on the chords of 'Cherokee', a piece so technically demanding that Gillespie took over the trumpet duties.

Almost 50 years later, Davis's contribution to the Parker quintet occasionally resurfaces as the subject of fundamental disagreement. It began with *Down Beat* magazine's review of the 78 rpm coupling of 'Billie's Bounce' and 'Now's the Time', published in April 1946, which contained a peremptory dismissal: 'The trumpet man, whoever the misled kid is, plays Gillespie in the same manner as a majority of the kids who copy their idol do – with most of the faults, lack of order and meaning, the complete adherence to technical acrobatics. . . .' There and then, a wounded young trumpeter began a lifelong distrust of critics. Even his fiercest defenders would hardly dispute that, had Miles Davis not developed his playing far beyond what we hear on these sides, he could never have turned into the significant figure he was to become. But his playing on this initial session with Parker's band was nevertheless full of care and thought, if not complete confidence or stylistic security. He may not have jousted with Parker as Gillespie did (and would do again on a handful of historic occasions), but his economy and comparative reticence made a charming foil for Parker's expansive eloquence, and the blend of his small but perky tone with the thicker, richer, more assertive sound of the alto in the unison theme statements set a pattern and a style for countless bop and post-bop sessions to come.

Davis stayed with Parker for three years, a time of ups and downs, ins and outs, dozens of club engagements of every complexion from divine to embarrassing, and quite a few distinguished recordings. Parker's drug habit made life difficult; there were dealers around at the 'Now's the Time' session and they rarely left him alone. Davis worshipped Parker's playing and admired his intellectual capacity, but found his personal habits tiresome and depressing.

Their first temporary separation came at Christmas 1945, when Parker and Gillespie were booked by the agent Billy Shaw into a long engagement at Billy Berg's Club in Hollywood. The vice squad had just raided 52nd Street, closing down several clubs and doing nothing for business at the remainder, which made New York look like a good place not to be for a while. California was still virgin territory for East Coast beboppers, although a fresh generation of black Los Angeles musicians had been listening to the new sounds and trying to emulate them in the clubs along Central Avenue. These young men, including the pianist Hampton Hawes, altoist Sonny

Fats Navarro (left),
Davis and trombonist
Eddie Bert (right) at
Birdland in January
1949. Navarro might
have been the
greatest of them all,
had heroin not
snuffed out his
incandescent talent.

Criss, trumpeter Art Farmer and drummer Roy Porter, gave the Parker–Gillespie raiding party a warm welcome, and the gig at Billy Berg's was a hit.

Davis, meanwhile, went back home to East St Louis with his young family to spend the Christmas holiday. (Irene was pregnant again, and their first son, Gregory, was born in 1946.) While he was there, the Benny Carter Orchestra arrived to play at the Riviera in St Louis. Davis crossed the river to say hello and found himself being offered a job with the band, which was based in Los Angeles. Hankering after a reunion with Parker, he agreed, and not long afterwards found himself playing after-hours sessions with Bird at the Finale Club in LA while fulfilling his commitment to Carter at the Orpheum Theatre. This double-dating was frowned on by the union, which fined him for the transgression of its rules and forced him to make a choice. It wasn't difficult. Davis had swiftly discovered that Carter's bread-and-butter arrangements bored him, and he left to rejoin Parker, who should have flown back to New York with Gillespie and the rest of the band but had cashed in his air ticket to buy heroin instead.

In March, Bird and Miles went into Radio Recorders on Santa Monica Boulevard with five other musicians and cut an important session for Dial Records, a new label set up by the promoter Ross Russell. These versions of 'Yardbird Suite', 'Ornithology' and 'Moose the Mooche', informally arranged

at the recording session itself, revealed a relaxed Parker at the height of his powers, although Davis's contribution was not particularly distinguished. Perhaps the highlight of the six-hour date was Parker's unaccompanied break on 'Night in Tunisia', a four-bar outburst into which he seemed to pour a lifetime's music, the alto saxophone no longer a mechanical thing of rods and springs and pads but an open tap from which molten music gushed in a superheated flood.

Parker was off heroin, but had started to drink to compensate. By July he was in a bad way. The trumpeter Howard McGhee, who had befriended Parker and Davis, tried to help him and took him back into the studio in an attempt to pull him together. This time the result was a disaster, and the 'Lover Man' session, as it became known, stands as an infamous documentary of the breakdown of a genius. It should have been destroyed, instead of being preserved to permit posterity to inspect an example of total artistic disintegration. That same night, Parker was committed to Camarillo State Hospital, where he spent the next seven months before returning to New York.

Davis filled the time in California by working with the tenorist Lucky Thompson, who had played on the 'Yardbird Suite' session, and the bassist and composer Charlie Mingus, a wild iconoclast who was then styling his ensemble 'Baron Mingus and his Symphonic Airs'. In September, help

At Birdland again, with the bassist Oscar Pettiford and pianist Bud Powell. The vibes (just visible behind Pettiford) are Milt Jackson's.

arrived in the shape, once again, of the Billy Eckstine Orchestra, now entering the final stretch of its financially beleaguered career. And, yet again, Davis was invited to replace a missing trumpeter – this time Fats Navarro, who had opted to stay in New York. Davis spent the next five months on the road with the band, until it broke up in Chicago in the spring of 1947.

Something else happened in those months, though. Having stayed clean through his first few years on the jazz scene, despite his proximity to Parker, Miles Davis now got involved with drugs. By his own account, he was turned on to cocaine by the trumpeter Hobart Dotson and to heroin by the tenorist Gene Ammons, both colleagues in the Eckstine band.

When he got back to New York, there was good news: *Esquire* magazine had named him as the new star trumpeter in its annual poll. There was also a job waiting: a couple of weeks with the Dizzy Gillespie Big Band at a theatre in the Bronx. Gillespie's outfit, formed the previous year, had picked up where the Eckstine mob left off. This, too, was a full 16-piece orchestra, playing advanced arrangements by Gil Fuller, Tadd Dameron, George Russell and others, a wildly combustible mix of Afro-Cuban rhythms – a special love of Gillespie's – and bebop techniques. For those few dates, Davis found himself alongside Dizzy, Fats Navarro, Freddie Webster and Kenny Dorham in a dream trumpet section. On opening night there was also the presence of Charlie Parker, but Gillespie fired the man he had once called 'the other half of my heartbeat' after Bird repeatedly nodded off on the stand, rousing himself only for his solos.

Nevertheless, Parker turned out to be Davis's next employer. A four-week stint with Bird's quintet – also featuring Max Roach, bassist Tommy Potter and pianist Duke Jordan – at the Three Deuces was so well received that the engagement was extended and then extended again. After his rehabilitation at Camarillo, Parker was using heroin again, but in every other respect this season was one of his most successful. It was important for Davis, too, because his work on the recordings made during this period show his musical character gradually forming itself, as his tone developed a finer focus and his ideas took a more definite shape. Throughout 1947 and 1948, the quintet – sometimes with Bud Powell on piano, occasionally with J.J. Johnson's trombone added to form a sextet – reeled off a series of recordings for Savoy and Dial that amounted to a statement of the formal perfection attainable within bebop. They may have lacked the thrilling raw edge that came in live performance (and which can be heard in the Dean Benedetti recordings from the Three Deuces and elsewhere, unearthed and issued during the late 1980s), but they displayed a control and maturity that silenced those who condemned the boppers as incompetent anarchists.

Davis, however, was growing restless. There were things about Parker that he loved, things that no one else could have given him. Parker was the most brilliantly gifted improviser in jazz history and his discoveries affected every jazz musician who came after him. Davis also admired his spontaneous approach to recording, which usually overcame the deadening effect of a cold studio climate. And Parker's attitude to the audience impressed a young musician anxious to find an alternative to the ingratiating Uncle Tom-style tactics of an earlier generation. Parker often didn't tell the audience what he was going to play, or what he had just played. He paid them the compliment of expecting them to work it out for themselves. The music was what it was, whatever that turned out to be; you didn't need to be told that it was a 12-bar blues or a variation on the changes of 'Sweet Georgia Brown' in order to get the point. That was just a waste of breath.

But there were also things that tried Davis's patience, notably Parker's perennial unreliability and his slipperiness over money. Miles was now the band's musical director, but he was beginning to feel that putting up with Parker's arrogance was not worth the trouble. Plus, underneath it all and exciting as it had been, bebop was a music created by a bunch of other fellows. It had given him a wonderful apprenticeship and earned him a reputation, but now Miles Davis had music of his own to invent.

The gig with Parker had brought Davis right into the public eye. By the end of 1948, he was starting to win magazine polls.

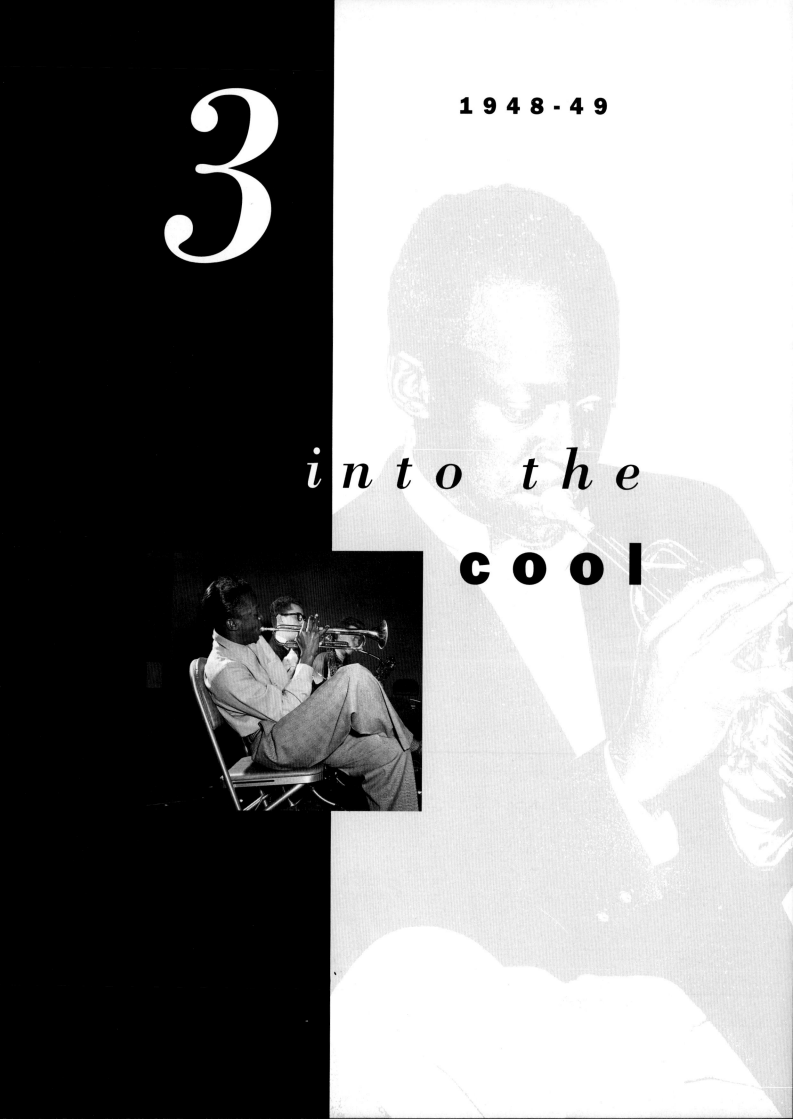

3

1948-49

into the

cool

in to the cool

the apartment was on West 55th Street, behind a Chinese laundry, and it belonged to Gil Evans, a Canadian-born arranger who had made a small reputation writing charts for the big band of pianist Claude Thornhill. Together, Evans and Davis were to exert a remarkable influence on post-war popular music, and Evans's apartment was where they laid their plans.

Evans had found Thornhill an unusually constructive employer during his first spell with the band in 1941–42, having been encouraged in his attempts to lead the ensemble away from the clichés of swing and into its own artistic territory. Both the leader and his arranger, who admired Ravel and Fauré just as much as he loved Armstrong and Ellington, were interested in unusual textures, so the band had been expanded to include a pair of French horns and a tuba, while the saxophone section made frequent use of a wide range of auxiliary reed and woodwind instruments, from piccolo to bass clarinet. Thornhill and Evans also shared a liking for music that avoided too much pace: like other bands, they played for dancers, but it must have

been hard to do anything other than smooch to Thornhill's largely slow-motion repertoire, with its panoply of rich inner voicings and exotic detailing. Inevitably, such a band could not outlast the boom years of the swing era; when Thornhill came out of the US Navy in 1946, he reassembled many of his old sidemen, together with some talented newcomers, but since even the likes of Goodman and Basie were feeling the pain as the post-war economy bit, there wasn't much hope for an overmanned and idiosyncratic outfit like Thornhill's. His prestige was unusually high, though, among musicians – although normally contemptuous of commercial big-band leaders, they recognised and applauded an unusual degree of altruism struggling against the odds in an unhelpful environment.

Not long before the band met its demise as a permanent unit in the late forties, Thornhill allowed Evans to add arrangements of three bebop pieces to its book. This was hardly the way to the feet of the average dance-hall crowd, or to the hearts of the coast-to-coast radio audience, and it must have symptomatic of Thornhill's disastrous commercial judgement. When the band recorded Evans's recastings of Parker's 'Yardbird Suite', 'Anthropology' and 'Donna Lee' late in 1947, it was clear that Evans had attempted to retain the fleetness and mobility of a bebop combo while fleshing out the tones and textures with the broader instrumental resources at his disposal. Two soloists of the younger generation, the alto saxophonist Lee Konitz and the trumpeter Red Rodney, contributed idiomatic solos, while the single overhanging tuba tones which closed both pieces on a note of irresolution were typical Thornhill, typical Evans and a very explicit foreshadowing of things to come.

Davis met Evans when the arranger came looking for a lead-sheet of 'Donna Lee' from which to work on the arrangement for Thornhill. A man of broad cultural interests and great (although diffident) charm, Evans immediately discovered a rapport with the young trumpeter. At 35, Evans was 14 years older than Davis, but his attitudes and enthusiasm were beyond considerations of age, as they remained until his death 40 years later. Davis found in his new friend a source of complementary knowledge, a natural wisdom and, perhaps most important, an impeccable sense of taste in all things.

After his apprenticeship with Parker, Davis was ready to move on, towards a more individual approach to the art of jazz. First came the question of what it was for. Since its early days on the streets of New Orleans, jazz had been a

At the Capitol studios with pianist Al Haig, who deputised for John Lewis.

Davis, Konitz and Mulligan: distinctive instrumental voices that blended to change the sound and style of jazz.

music with a strong component of competitive machismo, to which the Olympic motto of 'Faster, higher, stronger' could well have been applied. The trumpeter Buddy Bolden could be heard, according to legend, 30 miles away on a clear night; in Kansas City in the thirties, the ethos of the 'cutting contest' had turned improvisation into a trial of strength that had as much to do with staying power as with aesthetic judgement. For Davis, this was not enough. His competitive instinct, evident in his parallel love of sport, was not the sort that finds its satisfaction in the simple toe-to-toe trading of blows. His superiority could only be expressed in something far subtler: the development of a style, both personal and musical, so cool as to render its owner beyond competition – untouchable, unknowable, invulnerable.

The place to start was with the sound and the speed of the music, and it was here that Gil Evans could provide priceless help. In his new friend's work for the Thornhill band, Davis heard something that he could use: an elegance and sophistication to complement and enhance the feelings he had inside him. Evans could make music that was delicate without being effete, that could sing of the blues without needing to cover itself in sweat. Against that background, Davis could begin the true evolution of a voice that had had no room to grow within the brisk technical rigour of bebop. He was not like Armstrong or Parker, a soloist who

could define and carry the whole thing himself, irrespective of the type or quality of the supporting musicians. For him, totality was the key: the style, the setting, the mood. His individual contribution was the final touch, but it represented perhaps less than half of what he brought to the music. The rest was a sensibility, an awareness of possibilities, a perfect taste, a unique atmosphere.

To the dark, airless one-room basement on West 55th Street that summer of 1948 came a procession of restless, talented young musicians in search of the next step after bebop. Besides Evans and Davis there were John Lewis, 27, a calm, thoughtful pianist and composer who had worked with Parker and Gillespie, and would go on to become the guiding spirit of the Modern Jazz Quartet; Gerry Mulligan, 21, the crew-cut baritone saxophonist who had written 'Disc Jockey Jump' for the popular swing band of Gene Krupa and who was to lead one of the most influential small groups of the fifties; and George Russell, 24, a music professor's son who, during a lengthy period in hospital under treatment for tuberculosis, had formulated a new system of harmonic principles which he would later publish as the Lydian Chromatic Concept of Tonal Organisation. From their conversations and practical experiments, something new and important began to grow.

Evans had always liked the idea of writing for individual soloists. An ambition to work with Louis Armstrong foundered on the indifference of the trumpeter's manager, while his approach to Parker, although more warmly received, fell victim to Bird's unwillingness to concentrate on the longer term. In Davis, however, he found the perfect voice and an entirely complementary character.

Their plan was quickly settled: it called for a scaled-down version of the Thornhill band, retaining as far as possible its range of both pitch and timbre. In Davis's mind, the band would be structured in a way that would mimic the voicing of a vocal quartet: bass, baritone, alto and soprano. A rhythm section of piano, bass and drums would support six horns: trumpet and alto saxophone at the top, trombone and French horn in the middle, baritone saxophone and tuba below. What was immediately clear was that this formula would not lead the band to become a mere pocket version of the standard trumpets–trombones–saxophones big band set-up. Each horn had its own voice, and was deployed with a flexibility that permitted many different combinations. Most of all, there could be air and space between the voices.

As important as the instrumentation, though, was the specific identity of the musicians. The rhythm section comprised Lewis, the powerful bop bassist Al McKibbon and Max Roach, Parker's tough, brilliant drummer. Joining Davis and Mulligan in the horn chairs were a young trombonist, Mike

Zwerin; a French horn specialist, Junior Collins; and two graduates from the Thornhill academy, the tuba player Bill Barber and the alto saxophonist Lee Konitz. The presence of the latter was the subject of some controversy. Davis had wanted Sonny Stitt, a gifted Parker clone, to occupy the alto chair. Mulligan, however, insisted that Konitz's pale, featherweight tone and more oblique phrasing would provide a crucially different inner voice, whereas the presence of a Parkerish sound in combination with Davis's trumpet and the bop-based rhythm section would skew the overall sonority too far towards conventional modern jazz, when they were looking for something else altogether. Realising the truth of Mulligan's perception, Davis accepted Konitz's arrival and the group was ready to take its first steps.

They didn't have much in the way of a repertoire, since Evans was a notoriously slow worker and, in any case, everything had to be tailor-made to fit the unusual line-up. Mulligan and Lewis pitched in with arrangements, while Davis took upon himself the burden of organising rehearsals, calling the musicians and hustling for gigs. It was his first real shot at leadership, and he was making a serious effort to turn this extraordinary outfit into a credible working proposition. Monte Kay, an agent who worked with many jazz musicians, eventually booked the nine-piece ensemble into the Royal Roost on Broadway, where it opened in August

With the nonet at the Royal Roost on Broadway in 1949: the band was not a commercial success in its working lifetime, but it drew enough attention from fellow musicians to raise Davis's status.

1948, second on the bill to the Count Basie Orchestra, under a sign reading 'Miles Davis's Nonet: Arrangements by Gerry Mulligan, Gil Evans and John Lewis'. An unusual form of billing, this clearly established that the band's unique selling point was the unorthodox configuration of its ensemble.

The fortnight's engagement attracted the attention of some of the more inquiring minds among their fellow musicians. Basie himself listened and is reported to have told Davis that the band's music was 'slow and strange, but real good'. The critics were less certain, but Pete Rugolo, the musical director of Capitol Records, showed an interest. Since Rugolo, born in Sicily and raised in California, was himself a skilled arranger who had helped to establish the controversial 'progressive jazz' style of the Stan Kenton Orchestra in the mid-forties, his enthusiasm was hardly surprising: this was first and foremost an arranger's band. Recordings taken during the engagement demonstrate the band's confidence, notably with their adaptations from the bebop canon, such as Mulligan's swinging arrangement of 'Godchild', a serpentine medium-tempo line by the pianist George Wallington, and Lewis's straightforward orchestrations of Bud Powell's 'Budo' and Denzil Best's 'Move'. More adventurous was Lewis's recasting of 'S'il vous plaît', a pop song in which he split the horns into two sections, one moving in counterpoint at half the speed of the other. But the highlight of the

surviving tapes, and the piece which most clearly realised the nonet's ambitions, was Evans's only contribution: an arrangement of a commercial song called 'Moondreams' which began in a manner that would have been conventional enough for the Thornhill band – a gentle reverie floating on the slow 4/4 of Roach's brushes – but gradually accumulated a strange and intense luminosity until, in the final section, the tempo disappeared along with the rhythm section, the alto saxophone held a series of unearthly whistling high notes, the trumpet and the tuba wandered beneath it, the trombone stuttered and each voice appeared to be acting semi-autonomously until the piece tapered away in what might be called a constructive anti-climax. Nothing could have been closer to the spirit of the title: a moonstruck fantasy. And, apart from a few linking bars by Gerry Mulligan, there was no space at all for improvised solos; yet in a way the whole thing, every notated measure of it, had the freshness and spontaneity of improvisation, plus an intriguing indirectness that set it far apart from anything else to be heard on Broadway or 52nd Street that summer.

Rugolo could not take the nonet into the recording studio during or immediately after its engagement at the Royal Roost, since the American Federation of Musicians had instigated a recording ban which lasted throughout 1948. (It was breached by small independent labels, but not by majors

Capitol Records studios, New York, 21 January 1949: Junior Collins (French horn), Bill Barber (tuba), Kai Winding (trombone), Max Roach (drums, behind screens), Gerry Mulligan (baritone saxophone), Miles Davis (trumpet), Al Haig (piano), Lee Konitz (alto saxophone) and Joe Shulman (bass).

like Capitol.) There was no other interest from agents, so the project was put on hold and Davis worked around New York with a variety of musicians, including Fats Navarro, Bud Powell and the young tenor saxophonist Sonny Rollins. He also turned down an invitation to join the Duke Ellington Orchestra, flatteringly delivered by Ellington himself. In January 1949 he made his first visit to the recording studios since the end of the ban, for a date featuring the winners of the *Metronome* readers' poll. He had placed third in the trumpet category and joined the winner, Dizzy Gillespie, and the runner-up, Fats Navarro, plus the laureates of other instruments, including Parker, the trombonist Kai Winding, the extraordinary pianist Lennie Tristano and the drummer Shelly Manne in a celebratory Pete Rugolo composition called 'Overtime'. A few days later, at Rugolo's behest, the nonet was

42

With Max Roach at the Royal Roost during the nonet's first engagement in August 1948, second on the bill to Count Basie.

reconvened in a New York studio for the first of three dates that would change the sound of jazz.

The sessions took place over a period of 15 months and featured several musicians who had not been in the original line-up. Davis, Konitz, Mulligan and Bill Barber were the only constants; others who passed through included the drummer Kenny Clarke (an old acquaintance from Minton's), the trombonists Winding and J.J. Johnson, the pianist Al Haig, the French horn players Gunther Schuller and Sandy Siegelstein, and the bassists Joe Schulman and Nelson Boyd. Four titles were recorded at each session, and six of the total of 12 were released on 78 rpm singles: 'Move' coupled with 'Budo', 'Godchild'/'Jeru' and 'Boplicity'/'Israel', the last named a composition by the trumpeter John Carisi, another Thornhill alumnus introduced to the group by Evans. The remainder, including a vocal treatment of 'Darn That Dream' featuring the bebop singer Kenny Hagood, had to wait until later in the fifties, when they were collected in an album, titled *Birth of the Cool*, to see the light of day. Initially, public reaction was minimal; only Rugolo's enthusiasm kept the sessions coming. But, gradually, musicians across America began to pay attention to the smooth, serene approach of this strange little band. After the power of the big bands, the raw freneticism of jump music and the high-octane intensity of bebop, this new sound, practically weightless and with a porcelain surface, proposed an entirely different direction. Disdaining obvious effort and explicit emotional involvement, it suggested the obliqueness and detachment of a new kind of hipster.

Not everybody liked it. Dizzy Gillespie, for one, was ambivalent about the way it had discarded the heat of his kind of jazz: 'It didn't bother me because it came right out of what we'd been doing. It was just a natural progression because Miles had definitely come right out of us, and he was the leader of this new movement. So it was the same music, only cooler. They expressed less fire than we did, played less notes, less quickly, and used more space, and they emphasised tonal quality. This music, jazz, is guts. You're supposed to sweat in your balls in this music. They sorta softened it up a bit.'

For Davis, the music of Gillespie and Parker had simply been too complex for the mainstream audience to follow: 'If you weren't a fast listener, you couldn't catch the humour or feeling in their music. Their musical sound wasn't sweet, and it didn't have harmonic lines that you could easily hum out on the street with your girlfriend trying to get over with a kiss. Bird and Diz were great, fantastic, challenging, but they weren't sweet. But *Birth of the Cool* was different because you could hear everything, and hum it also. We shook people's ears a little softer than Bird or Diz did.'

The cool world was here.

4

1949-54

strung

out

Previous pages:

Left: Poll-winner:
with Ralph Burns
(trumpet) and Terry
Gibbs (vibes) at the
1951 *Metronome* All-
Stars session,
playing 'Local 802
Blues' — a
dedication to the
New York City branch
of the American
Federation of
Musicians.

Right: Having
organised the
nonet's rehearsals,
hustled for its gigs
and secured its
record deal, Davis
entered the fifties as
a fully fledged
leader.

It took years for the nonet's music to work its way through the system of American music. The heyday of its influence, in fact, was to be the mid-fifties, when practically every young arranger in California tried to emulate its breezy insouciance. For Davis, Evans, Lewis and their colleagues, however, the band's existence was compressed into 15 months, spanning the two-week engagement at the Royal Roost and three days in the studio for the Capitol sessions. Apart from rehearsals, that was it: the sum of the life of one of the most influential ensembles of post-war popular music.

If he was having trouble making an impact as the leader of an innovative band, Davis's reputation as a trumpeter was nevertheless on the upswing, and in May 1949 he and Tadd Dameron, the pianist and composer in whose bands he had sometimes appeared in New York, travelled to the Festival de Jazz in Paris. Over eight nights they shared the stage at the Salle Pleyel with Charlie Parker (whose quintet now featured Kenny Dorham, a Davis disciple, on trumpet), Sidney Bechet, the boogie pianist Pete

Johnson and an all-star mainstream band featuring the trumpeter Hot Lips Page and the tenorist Don Byas. To complete their own line-up, Davis and Dameron recruited three Paris-based musicians: two Americans – Kenny Clarke, the father of modern jazz drumming, and James Moody, a young tenor saxophonist who had played with the Gillespie big band in New York – and a French music student, the bassist Barney Spieler. Almost 30 years later, some of the quintet's performances from the festival were released on an album, showing that they gave the French audience a very straightforward, hard-driving account of bebop, trusting to such standard texts as Parker's 'Ornithology', Denzil Best's 'Allen's Alley' and Dameron's own 'Good Bait' and 'Lady Bird'.

For Davis, the significance of the trip – his first outside the United States – went beyond the music. The most eloquent pages of his autobiography deal with the revelation of a world outside America: a world where black and white didn't seem to constitute a division. 'I had never felt that way in my life,' he was to say. 'It was the freedom of . . .

being treated like a human being, like someone important.' And of meeting Juliette Gréco.

The archetypal Left Bank woman, with long black hair, big dark eyes, pale skin and a baggy sweater, Gréco was at 22 already a popular singer. She and Davis met backstage; the attraction was instantaneous, mutual and profound. For Davis, 'she taught me what it was to love someone other than music.' She was the first woman he had found himself loving as an equal. The impact of that can hardly be overestimated, all the more so in the context of springtime Paris and its adoring jazz fans flocking to the Salle Pleyel every night, making him believe that perhaps there was a society in which the colour of a man's skin did not predetermine his place in society, in which the music of the Afro-American could be the object of respect and study. Davis later claimed that Jean-Paul Sartre suggested he and Juliette should get married; a surprisingly mundane suggestion, perhaps, coming from the godfather of existentialism, but one that Davis resisted with the greatest difficulty. It was a decision he lived to regret.

Before May was out, full of misgivings, he had said goodbye to Gréco and returned to New York, still the testing ground of any jazz musician worthy of the name. Beside the clubs of 52nd Street, the *boîtes* of the Left Bank were a child's playpen. But America meant at best indifference, at worst outright racism. The result, for a 23-year-old trumpeter who had sampled a

better way of life, was a descent into a deep involvement with heroin. Of course, everyone was doing it – from Bird and Lady Day through Dexter Gordon and Sonny Rollins to Art Blakey and J.J. Johnson. Some, like his friends Freddie Webster and Fats Navarro, had died or would die in squalor from the destructive effects of the drug. Others, Blakey and Johnson among them, would clean themselves up and live long and happy lives, covered with honours. But for Davis at that moment, the combination of the example of his peers and America's lack of response to its most vital native art held sway. With Irene and the children in an apartment in Queens, Davis took to spending much of his non-playing time uptown, scoring smack and learning how to shoot up. He wasn't short of teachers.

Heroin, he was later to say, changed his entire personality. Living in the Hotel America on 48th Street, he began a second career as a pimp to make the money that would support his habit. In an attempt to break the cycle, he, Irene and the children drove home to East St Louis, where the finance company repossessed his car and the family settled in time for Irene to give birth to a third child, Miles IV.

By that time, though, Miles III was long gone – on the road with a new edition of the Billy Eckstine band, packed with fellow junkies. The tour ended in Los Angeles, where he was busted (set up, he claimed many years later, by Art Blakey) and spent a short

but unforgettable time in prison, pending charges. On his release, awaiting trial, he lived for a while with Dexter Gordon and struck up a friendship with Art Farmer, a gifted young LA-based trumpeter who was to absorb the essentials of Davis's trumpet style and transmute them into an approach of his own. A gig with Billie Holiday in Chicago preceded the trial in LA, where he was acquitted. But the publicity surrounding the arrest had done its job, and employers were wary of him.

Back in New York at the beginning of 1951, Davis recorded with Parker for Verve Records and, later the same day, cut his own first session for the small Prestige company, with which he had signed a non-exclusive contract. Unfortunately his health and physical condition weren't up to the workload, and his playing on his own date was among his most lacklustre efforts. Much better was his performance on a date led by Lee Konitz, who had fallen under the spell of the brilliant pianist and teacher Lennie Tristano, a man devoted to the admiration of Charlie Parker and Lester Young and to the development of a complex, emotionally restrained, harmonically based style of improvisation which formed another offshoot of the 'cool' phenomenon.

Davis was still being placed high in the polls, and had become a regular invitee to the *Metronome* All-Stars dates, but he was living the life of a junkie pimp, and when he got the call to lead his second Prestige date, that

Two young stars:
with tenorist Stan
Getz at the 1951
Metronome All-Stars
session. Like Davis,
Getz developed an
unmistakable sound
on his instrument.

October, he put together a band filled with fellow addicts: the young saxophonists Sonny Rollins and Jackie McLean, the pianist Walter Bishop Jr, and Blakey. Charlie Parker was present, and the mood was excited – particularly since Davis was told that the session would be released on an LP, and that he no longer needed to worry about making every piece conform to the three-minute limit of the old 78 rpm disc. This was effectively the moment at which he began his challenge to conventional ideas of the musical time-frame – a challenge which was to become the major preoccupation of popular music towards the end of the century, and one that would eventually link him with such contrasting creative forces as James Brown and Andy Warhol.

Some time in 1952, Davis's father – probably alerted by Clark Terry, whose clothes and trumpet Davis had tried to pawn in order to raise money for heroin – travelled to New York to find his son, persuaded him to terminate an engagement at the Downbeat Club and took him home on a train to East St Louis to sort himself out. Miles II went so far as to have his son arrested and taken to prison, but the treatment didn't take: within weeks Davis was back in New York, recording for Blue Note, another small jazz label, again with Jackie McLean on alto, plus J.J. Johnson on trombone and Kenny Clarke, briefly back from Paris, on drums. The music was crisp and confident, the trumpeter in command of his material, if not of his life.

That year, too, he employed the tenor saxophonist John Coltrane for the first time. The two had met some months earlier, when Coltrane was a member of the Dizzy Gillespie band. Coltrane joined Davis for a concert at the Audubon Ballroom, substituting for Jackie McLean alongside Rollins and Davis himself – and bringing together the men who were to form the twin polarities of tenor playing for the next decade and a half. The precocious 22-year-old Rollins, although three years younger than Coltrane, had the upper hand on the night, and it would be some years before Davis resumed his partnership with the shy Philadelphia-bred musician whose influence on jazzmen around the world would one day rival his own.

The big gig of 1952 was a nationwide tour with an all-star band under the non-playing leadership of 'Symphony Sid' Torin, a well-known jazz disc jockey who broadcast live from the Royal Roost in the forties and from Birdland in the fifties. Davis, the tenorist Jimmy Heath, J.J. Johnson, Kenny Clarke, the vibraphonist Milt Jackson and the bassist Percy Heath were the featured musicians; according to Davis, they didn't care much for the idea of travelling under the aegis of a man whose only instrument was the radio microphone and who took a fat cut of the money for his efforts.

Parker and Davis were briefly reunited in January 1953 for a Prestige session which featured Parker on tenor saxophone (as he had been for a Davis date for Savoy in 1947) alongside Rollins. But the real importance of the session resided in the presence of one Joseph Rudolph Jones, known to his friends as Philly Joe, a drummer from Philadelphia whose driving swing and extrovert sense of decoration and punctuation gave a new kind of momentum to the whole session, particularly to a serpentine Davis tune called 'Compulsion'.

A car trip to Los Angeles with Max Roach and Charlie Mingus that summer led to a meeting with a dancer named Frances Taylor, later to become Davis's first legal wife. First, though, after four years of immersion in the culture of heroin, during which time virtually every creative endeavour he had undertaken was in the society of fellow addicts, he had to kick it.

His father's guest house, on the farm outside East St Louis, formed the battleground. Locked inside for more than a week, he struggled with the craving, the uncontrollable sweating, the sheer physical pain experienced by a system deprived of its normal support. He wanted to scream. But, through the force of his own will, he emerged, almost clean.

Not quite, though. Six months in Detroit, attempting to stay away from the temptations of New York, introduced him to a generation of first-class local musicians, including the drummer Elvin Jones, the pianist Tommy Flanagan and the guitarist Kenny Burrell. It also allowed him to make the final effort to wean himself off this phase of his addiction, and by the time he returned to New York in February 1954 he was ready to put his career back on the tracks.

The most significant events of 1954 took place in the studio of the recording engineer Rudy Van Gelder in Hackensack, New Jersey, a short automobile ride from Manhattan, across the George Washington Bridge and up the turnpike. Van Gelder was a talented freelance who frequently worked for Prestige and Blue Note. Not only did his microphones capture the instruments with a clarity and warmth previously unheard in jazz recordings, but the atmosphere of his room seemed to relax the musicians who gathered there. In April, Davis convened the tenor saxophonist Lucky Thompson, the trombonist J.J. Johnson, the pianist Horace Silver and the Modern Jazz Quartet rhythm team of Percy Heath and Kenny Clarke; the sextet recorded a couple of tunes which are now seen as marking the birth of the idiom known as hard bop – the third wave of modern jazz, following on from bebop and cool.

A reaction against the adoption of cool jazz by the white West Coasters, hard bop was nevertheless far less frenetic than bebop. Although (as its name suggests) it rarely lacked aggression, its power was not always on full-frontal display. The suggestion of muscle was usually enough. Crucially, the format of the new 10-inch and 12-inch long-playing records now permitted soloists to stretch themselves over several choruses, pacing their improvisations to the rhythm of a longer cadence. This promoted relaxation and a sense of space; certainly nothing like Richard Carpenter's 'Walkin' ', a medium-tempo 12-bar blues from the April session, could have been attempted before. Stretching out over 13 minutes enabled the laconic quality of this simple tune to grow into a full-blown atmosphere.

Davis's gathering personal renaissance was given added impetus during the year by the release of an album containing most of the nonet's studio material, for which Capitol coined a title that came to stand for an entire genre, a whole generation and even others beyond them. *Birth of the Cool* is one of those fortunate phrases so evocative that every day an advertising copywriter or a headline sub-editor somewhere in the world is making use of its resonance.

But it was on Christmas Eve 1954 that the sound and shape of the future became truly apparent. To Rudy Van Gelder's that day travelled Davis, Milt Jackson, Thelonious Monk, Percy Heath and Kenny Clarke, all mature musicians and strong characters. The 56 minutes of music they recorded that day represent a milestone in jazz, a moment of rare perfection.

For Miles Davis, here at last was the unveiling of the sound that became the most immediately identifiable of musical signatures. From its uncertain beginnings, his trumpet tone had been developing body and shape. It had never really sounded like anyone else's – even that of his idol as far as timbre went, the late Freddie Webster; now, though, it suddenly came into full bloom. It seemed to be composed of opposing qualities: it was modest in size and yet rich in sonority; it was as pure as a boy soprano yet wreathed in pale smoke; it held the listener at a distance yet promised deep emotion. And there was more than just the sound: the shapes of Davis's improvised melodies were carved into the air so effectively that they seemed to hang for seconds, leaving a powerful after-image. His pacing, too, had changed. Gone was the bebopper's rush to get everything in. Now a sense of economy was the prevailing factor: each phrase was allowed time to breathe, time to claim a life in the listener's memory almost before it was over.

There were other potent factors in the success of the Christmas Eve date. First was the discreet smoothness of the Clarke/Heath rhythm section, which swung with matchless ease while leaving a clear track for the soloists. Second was the brilliance of Milt Jackson, whose blend with Davis in the theme statements was as important to the sound of the date as the excellence of his declamatory solos. Third was the tetchy relationship between the leader and his pianist: for Davis, Monk was a brilliant composer and pianist whose fondness for asymmetry – the sudden leap, the unexpected pause – nevertheless made him a liability as an accompanist. Throughout the trumpet solos on 'Bags'

Groove', for instance, Monk was nowhere to be heard; at Davis's insistence, he was keeping out of the trumpeter's way. This had the double virtue of permitting Davis as much clear space as he could handle, while also ensuring a moment of high drama when, under Jackson's vibes, the great pianist made his first, inimitable contribution.

After the Prestige sessions of 1954, nothing in jazz would sound quite the same. On the calm surfaces of 'Bags' Groove', 'The Man I Love' and 'Swing Spring' lay a reflection of the future.

The hands of a horn-player: New York, early fifties.

5

1955-57

the first **quintet**

three months into 1955, Charlie
Parker died. The bebop era was at
an end. In fact it had been over since the
day of the *Birth of the Cool* band's first
rehearsal, but it took the demise of its
presiding genius to make the closure
official. In early June, a few weeks after
Parker's death, Miles Davis went into
the studio to make a record that
expressed his personal conception, one
that owed little to collaborators. *The
Miles Davis Quartet*, as the album was
titled by Prestige, featured Philly Joe
Jones, the part-Choctaw, part-Cherokee
bassist Oscar Pettiford, and a 32-year-old
pianist from Dallas, Texas, called Red
Garland, who came recommended by
Philly Joe – and also, at least in Davis's
eyes, by his former career as a
professional boxer. Garland had a brisk,
swinging touch and a fondness for
passages played in jabbing block chords;
but he was also willing to bend his
approach to Davis's ideas of how things
should be done, which at this stage
involved a serious study of the work of
one Ahmad Jamal.

Born Fritz Jones in Pittsburgh in 1930,
Jamal was a precocious piano virtuoso
who led a trio based in Chicago. Since
1952 he had been making regular club
appearances in New York, where he
gathered a coterie of admirers. His touch
was light, never overbearing, in keeping
with his fondness for leaving plenty of
space within the trio's readings of
standard songs. He had a particular
liking for setting medium-tempo ballads
against a long-striding two-beat rhythm
in the bass – a habit which, when
assimilated by Miles Davis, became
almost universal among modern jazz
musicians. Jamal was not universally
acclaimed; admirers of more muscular
keyboard styles accused him of
effeteness, of being not much more than
a cocktail-lounge pianist. But space and
understatement were qualities Miles
Davis could respond to, and it was not
surprising that the new quartet album
contained versions of two songs, 'Will
You Still Be Mine' and 'A Gal in Calico',
which were part of Jamal's own
repertoire. Subsequently Davis was to
borrow many more of Jamal's favourite
tunes, notably 'But Not For Me', 'The
Surrey With the Fringe on Top', 'It
Could Happen to You', 'Spring is Here'

and 'On Green Dolphin Street', the theme tune from an obscure detective movie, which – transmitted to the world through Davis, via Jamal – became a hard bop standard.

In this exposed setting, too, it became even more evident that Miles Davis had acquired a unique signature: the solitary, moody, pensive sound – as the critic Kenneth Tynan's daughter was later to say – of 'a little boy who's been locked out and wants to get in'. And in July 1955, at the second Newport Jazz Festival, in the grounds of the old Lorillard mansion on Rhode Island, that signature inscribed itself on the consciousness of a wider audience. As part of an all-star band including Zoot Sims, Gerry Mulligan, Thelonious Monk, Percy Heath and Connie Kay, Davis played a muted ballad solo on Monk's 'Round Midnight' that brought the house down. The purity of the open horn, as heard on 'Bags' Groove', was one thing; the muted sound, a tight buzzing, suggested an even more intense and claustrophobic loneliness.

Such an impact did this appearance make that Davis won the *Down Beat* readers' poll as the top trumpeter at the end of 1955. There was an irony in the identity of the man he dethroned, the winner in 1953 and '54: Chet Baker, the young white musician who had made an impact with Gerry Mulligan's celebrated 'pianoless quartet' in 1952 and had gone on to become the leader of his own combo. Baker, whose playing also favoured the middle and lower registers

and conveyed an appealing impression of melancholy and vulnerability, had been deeply influenced by Davis; he, too, had no interest in the macho pyrotechnics of the Gillespie school. An intuitive musician who knew little of theory, Baker was an individualist rather than an innovator. Inevitably, Davis resented his commercial success, which was seen as that of a white man diluting the music's purity in order to make it palatable to a wider, less discriminating audience.

Now Davis was ready to launch his own regular working group. Like Parker, he opted for a quintet, the extra horn providing variety in both theme statements and solos. Philly Joe Jones and Red Garland were his first recruits, along with Paul Chambers, a 20-year-old bassist from Detroit whose playing had a mobility and firmness that made it the next step in the instrument's evolution from Jimmy Blanton through Oscar Pettiford. Chambers could make his walking 4/4 lines swing with a perfect combination of urgency and relaxation, and he could also imbue them with the sort of harmonic and melodic richness that would stimulate a soloist's imagination.

The first choice for a front-line partner was Sonny Rollins, still only 26 years old, whose reputation as one of the most intellectually and technically formidable of modern tenorists was growing fast. Rollins, though, was reluctant to commit himself to the project; it turned out that he wanted to commit himself to hospital instead, with

At the first Columbia Records session, with producer George Avakian.

the first quintet

the intention of kicking his heroin habit. To take his place, Philly Joe Jones put forward the name of John Coltrane.

It was his partnership with Coltrane that first gave Davis a reputation as a talent-spotter of unparalleled perspicacity, but his initial reaction to Jones's suggestion was one of scepticism. He remembered the earnest young tenorist being overshadowed by Rollins at the Audubon Ballroom in 1952, and he didn't see that as the best of auguries. After his stint with Gillespie's orchestra and quintet, Coltrane had subsequently played in the bands of Earl Bostic and Johnny Hodges; now he was about to take a gig with the organist Jimmy Smith in Philadelphia. Needing a second horn for the band's first engagement, in Baltimore that September, Davis gave in and let Jones call Coltrane – who announced himself ready to relinquish the Smith gig in favour of the greater musical challenge offered by Davis's new adventure.

Very soon, Davis realised how lucky he had been in his enforced choice of partner. 'Faster than I could have imagined,' he said of the new quintet, 'the music that we were playing together was just unbelievable.'

At its root was a wonderful rhythm section which really did sound like three parts of the same organism. First and foremost, Garland, Chambers and Jones took care not to duplicate each other's functions. There was no unison hammering of the beat. Chambers's gliding walk, Jones's sizzling ride cymbal

and commanding snare-drum commentary and Garland's urbane interjections dovetailed with such perfection that the impression was always of grace and light, even when the band was cooking hard on a bop tune.

But it was the contrast between the two horns that really set audiences talking. Davis's cool lyricism, even in its newly matured form, was essentially a known quantity, but Coltrane was a surprise to everyone. First there was his sound: a harsh, flat, intransigent tone, as dark as slate, that bore no evident relationship whatsoever to such established reference points of the tenor saxophone as Coleman Hawkins, Ben Webster, Lester Young or Dexter Gordon. In fact Young and Gordon were Coltrane's immediate forebears, but to say that this was not immediately obvious is an understatement. The emotional climate of Coltrane's playing, bleak and introspective, was something completely new to jazz; already, he had broken away.

The band discovered itself on the road, a tour through Detroit, Chicago and St Louis confirming in the minds of the musicians that here was something special, something much more than just another pick-up outfit. By the time they reached New York, Sonny Rollins was out of treatment, but Davis now considered Coltrane to be a fixture, and the quintet caused a sensation at the Café Bohemia in Greenwich Village.

Among the audience at the Bohemia most nights was George Avakian, an

The perfect silhouette: Stockholm, 1956.

A & R man for Columbia Records, the most powerful of America's major companies. In those days, Columbia prided itself on signing only the most significant artists in any field; to be a Columbia recording artist was to be ranked alongside Leopold Stokowski and Leonard Bernstein, Benny Goodman and Count Basie. In every sense, it was several leagues above the world represented by the small independent labels like Savoy, Prestige and Blue Note, who could offer only minimal fees, erratic royalty accounting and hurried recording sessions. (Although even here, standards could vary; it was often said that the difference between a Prestige session and a Blue Note was a day's rehearsal, since Blue Note's owners, Alfred Lion and Francis Wolff, were as meticulous about preparation as their funds would allow.) A company like Columbia could afford to spend money in and out of the studio: on arrangements, on orchestras, on sleeve art, on national distribution, on promotion to radio disc jockeys and the press. So when Miles Davis signed a contract with Columbia during the New York engagement, it marked perhaps the most significant step in his career since he tracked down Charlie Parker at the Heatwave Club that night in 1944.

There was a hitch, though: his Prestige contract still had a year to run, and it was agreed that he would record four albums' worth of material over the next year in order to bring the deal to a conclusion. For Prestige's Bob Weinstock, it was a wise move: he must have realised that the albums released on his label would benefit by association from Columbia's high-budget marketing, giving them in effect a free ride to a higher sales bracket. The material for Prestige turned out to be first rate, and became the series of albums known as *Steamin'*, *Workin'*, *Cookin'* and *Relaxin'*. The quintet tackled a remarkable variety of compositions, from pop songs like 'Diane' and 'Sweet Sue' through Broadway tunes like 'If I Were a Bell' and 'Bye Bye Blackbird' to pure jazz pieces like Benny Golson's 'Stablemates' and Sonny Rollins's 'Oleo'. While the rhythm trio set new standards, the horns offered their extraordinary hard-and-soft contrast.

Davis began recording his first Columbia album in the summer of 1956, during a long return engagement at the Café Bohemia. When it was released later that year, everything changed. *'Round About Midnight*, as it was called, boasted a sleeve photograph in which the trumpeter, head bowed, eyes invisible behind stylish oval-framed shades, was bathed in a wash of red light. It was the image that began to establish his mystique, his aloofness. Looking at this, anyone could tell that Miles Davis was not just another bebop trumpet player. With his substantial advances against royalties, he began to heighten the image by indulging his liking for stylish clothes and European sports cars: a white Mercedes was an early acquisition, the forerunner of a string of Ferraris and Lamborghinis which he updated at regular intervals over the next 30 years.

Around this time, too, Davis underwent the first of several operations to remove growths on his larynx. Ordered not to raise his voice for a couple of weeks while the post-operative healing was taking place, he nevertheless

With the tenorist Lester Young in Stockholm, 1956. Both developed light, flowing styles that ran against the grain but were eventually imitated the world over.

got into an argument with a music business executive, and shouted himself hoarse – permanently. The Miles Davis croak, the sound of a four-packs-a-day terminal case, became just another part of the growing legend. With its hint of menace, the voice also became a useful weapon in his dealings with club owners, whose demands he was starting to resist. Higher fees for himself and his sidemen, plus a stipulation of three sets a night, instead of the customary four, were among his significant victories. The owners and promoters began to realise that here was a man not afraid to face them down. If they refused to accede to his requirements, he would simply withhold his music.

Cunningly, the opening track on Davis's first Columbia release was the Monk ballad which had earned him such acclaim at Newport the previous year. The remainder of the album was the sort of mixed bag that might have made up the quintet's typical night-club set: Parker's 'Ah-leu-cha', Dameron's 'Tadd's Delight', Cole Porter's 'All of You', 'Bye Bye Blackbird' and 'Dear Old Stockholm', a Swedish folk song popularised in a jazz context by Stan Getz. The two-beat approach was shown off in the ballads, and every tune sounded as though it had been run in by a working band. The polish and confidence of the performance set the album apart from its Prestige predecessors, showing that Miles Davis was now a high-budget musician, ready to fulfil Columbia's expectations.

Life was not all smooth inside the quintet, though, despite the rave notices and fashionable audiences they were beginning to draw everywhere. Davis grew impatient with the band's indulgence in drink and drugs. They were all at it, in their different ways. One night late in 1956, Coltrane and his employer came to blows backstage in a New York nightclub – a scene witnessed by Thelonious Monk, who immediately offered Coltrane a job in his quartet. That time the tenorist stayed with Davis, but in March 1957 he was fired for real and joined Monk for a season at the Five Spot in New York, during which he cleaned himself up, concentrated on his playing, and turned himself from an interesting but immature musician into a fully formed innovator. Philly Joe was out, too. Their replacements were Sonny Rollins and Art Taylor, both fine musicians, but the mechanism of the band – its character, which depended on the individual personalities – was disrupted. For a while, the Belgian tenorist Bobby Jaspar replaced Rollins, who left to start his own band, and Tommy Flanagan took over from Red Garland. When Davis decided that Taylor's drumming wasn't hip enough, Jimmy Cobb, a 29-year-old drummer from Washington who had accompanied Billie Holiday, was ushered into his seat.

Beneath these changes, though, deeper currents were flowing. When they found expression, it was through the agency of two of his old friends, Gil Evans and Juliette Gréco.

**Backstage in
Stockholm in 1956,
with Milt Jackson.**

6

six of

one

Stay ahead: that was Miles Davis's guiding principle. Most jazz musicians are concerned only with the expression of their own character via their instrument in a setting determined by the particular genre in which they happen to operate. Others, rather fewer in number, are composers or arrangers, who control the setting in which the players are deployed. And there is a third category, which has no name. That is where Miles Davis belonged.

Davis became a great improviser, one of the most original and creative jazz has known, in the middle fifties. He was always a competent composer, although never a truly outstanding one. But the secret of his greatness lay in his insistence on keeping the music he played in a constant state of evolution, in his belief that what was said and how it was being said were the same thing. The driving force of this visionary impulse was a combination of his intellectual inquisitiveness and, more important, his permanent desire to be a leader. This meant taking upon himself the responsibility for the constant reconceptualisation of his music.

His friendship with Gil Evans, the most important of the three collaborators who had a significant impact on his career, had already led him into a kind of orchestral jazz that was not reliant on the stale patterns of big band music, as laid down by the likes of Fletcher Henderson and Count Basie in the early thirties and turned by the swing era into a desperately predictable formula. By the middle fifties, though, a group of young jazz-rooted composers was working on a new kind of music that might blend the swing and spontaneity of jazz with the greater instrumental and formal resources of classical music. The guiding light of this ambitious and eventually ill-fated movement was Gunther Schuller, a French horn player, composer and conductor who founded something called the Jazz and Classical Music Society in order to propagate the fusion he christened Third Stream music. With a grant from Brandeis University, Schuller commissioned compositions from J.J. Johnson, John Lewis, George Russell, Jimmy Giuffre, Charles Mingus, Milton Babbitt and others. When Columbia agreed to record

Rendezvous with Juliette Gréco in Paris, 1957: she introduced him to the young new-wave film director Louis Malle.

the pieces at the end of 1956, Davis was persuaded to take part as the featured soloist on two compositions: Johnson's 'Poem for Brass' and Lewis's 'Three Little Feelings', accompanied by 16 brass players and a three-piece rhythm section. Johnson's composition, rather portentous in tone and somewhat reminiscent of Stan Kenton's earlier experiments in 'progressive jazz', contained space for a short but effective medium-tempo solo by Davis, who was exploiting the warmer, softer sound of flügelhorn for the first time on record. Lewis's work, a characteristically delicate invention by the leader of the newly successful Modern Jazz Quartet, displayed a better grasp of the sort of setting that might inspire the star soloist. For Davis, though, the whole thing felt too rigid. He wanted to be trying something different, but whatever it was had to retain the core qualities of Afro-American music, rather than becoming compromised by the stiffness and formality of the Eurocentric straight world. The attention of the straights was worth having if it meant that jazz musicians were being given respect, but not at the expense of the music's soul.

It was Gil Evans who found a solution. At the end of 1956, Davis visited Europe for concerts in Paris, Stockholm and Amsterdam in a package including Lester Young, Bud Powell, the MJQ and the French pianist René Urtreger. As soon as he returned to New York, he and Evans threw themselves into a project that was to bring Davis a

new and far wider audience.

For the album, which was released under the title *Miles Ahead*, Evans prepared a suite of 10 compositions, drawn from various sources – John Carisi, Kurt Weill, Ahmad Jamal, Delibes, Dave Brubeck, J.J. Johnson, Bobby Troup, Davis and Evans themselves – which he arranged for a 19-piece band resembling a blown-up version of the *Birth of the Cool* nonet. With five trumpets, four trombones, two French horns, a tuba, one alto saxophone, one bass clarinet and two woodwind, plus bass and drums, all the 'voices' of the nonet were available for expansion and recombination.

But no one hearing *Miles Ahead* for the first time would have wasted time thinking about technical matters. They would have been too busy being ravished by the unearthly loveliness of the sound. So skilfully had Evans refurbished and linked his material that the whole thing sounded like a continuous concerto for flügelhorn and orchestra. Despite the evidence of various rather primitive tape-edits, a mood was created and held all the way from Carisi's hard-swinging 'Springsville', with its demanding high-register trumpet passages, to the dancing pop song 'I Don't Wanna Be Kissed By Anyone But You', travelling via the territories of melancholy, wistfulness and a sweetness that was never sentimental. In 'Blues for Pablo' and 'The Meaning of the Blues', Evans and Davis discovered new colours within the blues: a palette of delicate but resolute emotions, freshly mixed.

It was Evans's gift to make a 19-piece orchestra sound like a small combo. Sometimes, as in 'I Don't Wanna Be Kissed', he achieved the effect through letting the bass (Paul Chambers) and drums (Art Taylor) play just as they would with the quintet, while the orchestra added harmonic punctuation like a bigger version of Red Garland's piano. Through Evans's pencil – and under his baton – the big band sounded completely flexible and manoeuvrable. This was the wonderful illusion, and the

With George Avakian (and Lee Konitz, in the background) during the sessions for the album *Miles Ahead*.

key to the music's unique appeal: the orchestral writing sounded improvised, while Davis's improvisations attained such a pitch of formal perfection that they could have been pre-composed. *Miles Ahead* was greeted with rapture by critics and fans alike: unmistakably stylish and modern, simultaneously beautiful and demanding, it was recognised straight away as the first real step forward in orchestral jazz since the great Ellington band of the early forties.

During the summer, while *Miles Ahead* was awaiting release, Davis reconvened the quintet for a season at the Café Bohemia, with Rollins, Garland, Chambers and Taylor. Coltrane was not far away, over at the Five Spot on Cooper Square, in the Bowery, attending finishing school with Thelonious Monk. Unofficial recordings from the Bohemia show how much more ordinary the quintet sounded with Rollins and Taylor: the strange, compelling contrast of timbre and temperament between trumpet and tenor were much missed, along with the internal tension to which it contributed.

There are at least three versions of the story of how Miles Davis came to provide the music for the soundtrack of *Ascenseur pour l'échafaud* (Lift to the Scaffold), the 1957 black-and-white thriller by the young French film director Louis Malle, which starred Lino Ventura and Jeanne Moreau. Soundtracks are not usually seen as the vehicle for musical innovation; in this case, however, an apparently

Davis, Marcel
Romano and Louis
Malle discuss the
soundtrack for
*Ascenseur pour
l'échafaud.*

insignificant assignment became one of the pivotal moments of Davis's career.

The first version comes from Marcel Romano, a French promoter who booked Davis for a European tour in the last month of 1957. The tour turned out to be a mere five concerts – two in Paris, one each in Amsterdam, Stuttgart and Brussels – plus a week at the Club St Germain in Paris. Romano also planned to film the tour, even hiring a cinematographer, Jean-Claude Rappeneau, but the project fell through at the last minute. According to Romano, Rappeneau then mentioned that he was working on a feature film with Malle, and suggested that he should put Davis's name forward for the soundtrack. One of Davis's biographers, Ian Carr, claims that Malle, a long-time

Posing for a publicity shot with Jeanne Moreau, the star of Malle's movie.

Davis fan, actually went to the airport to meet Davis on his arrival and asked him there and then to contribute music to the film. Davis's own account was that once back in Paris he re-established his relationship with Juliette Gréco, who introduced him to Malle – who was indeed a fan, and immediately issued the invitation.

Whatever the truth (which is probably a combination of all three), Davis and his pick-up band found themselves in the Poste Parisien recording studios late on the night of 4 December. In a darkened room, Malle projected a loop of the sequences requiring music, while Davis and the other musicians improvised with their eyes on the screen. Far from feeling that his artistry was compromised or demeaned by such a functional attitude

to music, Davis looked on it as a challenge and a stimulus. His approach was to give the musicians a couple of chords and a tempo, and then to improvise. Of the 10 separate tracks that were eventually used, nine are based on the same two chords, D minor and C7; the tenth is a variation on the harmonic sequence of 'Sweet Georgia Brown', a popular vehicle for jazzmen. But the nine provided evidence of perhaps the most profound and remarkable of the changes that Miles Davis would impose on his music: the paring down of harmonic material practically to nothing.

Jazz had developed from popular songs and the blues, with their repeating 12-bar or 32-bar chord sequences. Bebop had revelled in extending the variety and complexity of those chords to the point that soloing over them had become more of a technical test than the invention of spontaneous melody, which is what it was supposed to be. Davis, to whom music had never represented a form of intellectual callisthenics, wanted to change the pace and register of the whole thing, and by this point the simplest way seemed to be to cut down the chords and to do away with the 'closed' structures. As a result, the soundtrack of *Ascenseur pour l'échafaud* took on a completely novel flavour, one that Davis would spend some years exploring.

Encouraged by the images on the screen, Davis created an unusually graphic mood: listening to the soundtrack in isolation, to the pieces eventually titled 'L'assassinat de Carla', 'Sur l'autoroute' and 'Au bar du petit bac', the listener has little difficulty summoning fugitive images of rain-washed Paris streets at dawn, of empty night-clubs, of lonely figures prowling the shadows. It isn't just the artificial echo which the engineer added to the natural sound: the untreated versions, released many years later, show that the music has a special atmosphere emanating not from its surface but from its essence. Never had Davis's music been so poised and assured, so stark and so spare; and the starker and sparer it became, the more power it exerted. This was the realisation towards which he had been working; now he had got there, it would condition every note he played. During an assignment that to another musician might have been merely a hack

job, Miles Davis had discovered the true characteristics – tragic, solitary, impenitent – of his artistic make-up.

He was lucky, though, in the choice of Paris-based musicians to accompany him on the concerts and, therefore, in the studio. Kenny Clarke, the most contented of expatriates, was on drums. Barney Wilen, a brilliant 20-year-old from Nice, was the tenor saxophonist.

Listening to a playback during the *Milestones* sessions, with pianist Red Garland.

Two more Frenchmen, the pianist René Urtreger and the bassist Pierre Michelot, slotted in perfectly, displaying a complete command of the modern jazz idiom and an obvious relish for the less familiar challenges Davis set them. Fortunately, too, some of the concert material was preserved, demonstrating the group's more conventional virtues on pieces such as 'Bags' Groove', 'Four' and 'A Night in Tunisia', and throwing into even sharper relief the extraordinary nature of the soundtrack.

Back in New York in the middle of December, Davis began to put into action a scheme he had been planning for more than a year. A young alto saxophonist from Florida, Julian 'Cannonball' Adderley, had made a big impact at the Café Bohemia and elsewhere. A bright, vivacious, garrulous player whose special affinity with the blues seemed to have been handed down from the jump-band players of the thirties and forties, Adderley made an unusually direct emotional appeal to the audience, bringing some of the rhetorical qualities of a gospel preacher to the

Cannonball Adderley, Miles Davis and John Coltrane at Newport, July 1958: did any jazz combo ever boast a more formidable front line? Paul Chambers is the bassist.

Garland, Davis, Chambers, Adderley: with *Milestones*, the sextet ushered in a new era.

language of bebop. Davis recognised that his broad tone and aggressive but essentially optimistic temperament could add a dimension to the quintet.

Coltrane had finished his stint with Monk, and was keen to return. So were Garland, Chambers and Jones. Around Christmas, the new Miles Davis Sextet played its first engagement, at the Sutherland Lounge in Chicago. Immediately, Davis knew he had found something special.

In March he was in Rudy Van Gelder's studio – not on his own behalf but as a special guest on an Adderley session, in a quintet completed by the pianist Hank Jones, bassist Sam Jones and drummer Art Blakey. The album was released under the title *Somethin' Else*, and until the eighties, when he began showing up on records by young pop groups, this was Davis's last appearance as a sideman in a small group. But although Adderley's name topped the bill on the sleeve, Davis's presence dominated the music. The first track, 'Autumn Leaves', made that clear. First, it was one of his borrowings from

the collected works of Ahmad Jamal. Second, it's hard to believe that he wasn't thinking, as he eased the theme through his tightly muted trumpet, of his most recent parting from Gréco; she had become closely identified with the song, in its original form, singing the Jacques Prévert lyric to 'Les feuilles mortes'. Here, under Adderley's name but treated with a subdued intensity that virtually defined Davis's mature aesthetic, was another classic reading.

Less than a month later, the time had come to record the sextet. Over two days, in Columbia's studios on Seventh Avenue, they taped the album that became known as *Milestones*, after its most famous track. It was with this album that Miles Davis finally established himself at the head of the field.

He had written a tune called 'Milestones' once before: a bebop tune for the 1947 Savoy session on which Charlie Parker played tenor. This new 'Milestones', though, was completely different. Here Davis formalised the discoveries he'd made while recording the soundtrack for Louis Malle. The harmonic movement was reduced to a bare minimum, the overt momentum provided by the energy of Chambers's fast-striding bass and Jones's smooth, even ride cymbal embellished with something that became known as the 'Philly lick': a rimshot tagging the fourth beat of each bar, marking off the journey like telegraph poles going by the window of a speeding car on a lonesome highway.

Jazz, being an art based on the organisation of the improvised, necessarily flirts with hit-and-miss; even its masterpieces often have unfinished edges. 'Milestones', though, was one of those rare pieces of jazz to which one could attach the adjective 'perfect' without any fear of contradiction. It lasted five minutes and 38 seconds, and not a note played by any of the six men in the course of that time could have been improved in any respect. It had mood, it had substance, it had edge, it had serenity, it had adventure, it had beauty. The theme, with Davis's open horn cruising in the clear air above the grainy blend of the saxophones and the calm push of Garland's piano chords, painted pictures straight away. With only half a beat's pause for breath, Adderley's opening solo came surging out in an unquenchable flood of melody: the blues as a music of joy and celebration, bursting with rhythmic energy. Then Davis, picking up Adderley's final phrase, entering his solo with calm control, his natural economy heightening the emotion of his ideas, floating little soft notes on the implacable current of the rhythm section, every now and then finding a phrase to redouble the momentum, like a boxer putting together a combination punch. And finally, after the effervescence of Adderley and the aloofness of Davis, the intensity of Coltrane, in turn mimicking the flügelhorn's final phrase and darkening the air with that great gaunt tone,

New York, 1958: Davis framed by Adderley's alto and Chambers's bass.

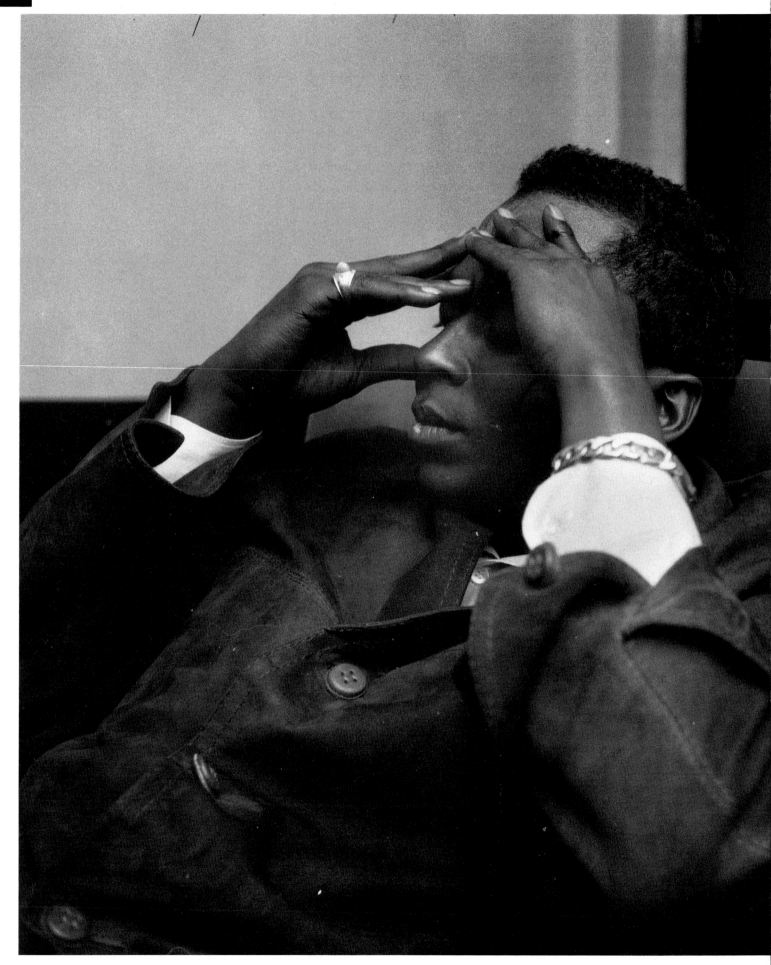

Playback at
Columbia: the sextet
and orchestral
albums alternated to
provide an unfolding
portrait of an
innovator at the
height of his
potency.

speeding across the surfaces of the tune, adjusting to the sudden changes of camber and leaving harsh tracks on its gentle inclines. There were no other solos to relieve the tautness of 'Milestones': just alto, trumpet and tenor, their contributions so exquisitely formed that they could be transcribed and taught in class. And then back to the theme, Philly Joe ticking off the telegraph poles beside the passing horns, eventually fading into the distance – an electronic fade-out, rare in the 'natural' world of acoustic jazz in the late fifties, but in this case a perfectly appropriate artistic device, demonstrating Davis's ability to conceive of a piece as something more than just a tune with solos. The structural integrity of 'Milestones' was unbreachable, the ideal marriage of form and content; no doubt Gil Evans had some inspirational role in its conception, for it achieved many of his objectives, and with very limited instrumental resources. There is a universe in 'Milestones', and the more often it is played, the more compelling it becomes.

The remainder of the album was a portrait of a superlative working band. Hard bop classics like Jackie McLean's 'Dr Jackle' and Monk's 'Straight, No Chaser' were pulverised by the triple-threat front line, while Davis allowed Garland to lead a trio version of the folk song 'Billy Boy' – once again an explicit salute to Jamal, who had recorded it himself in 1951. But this was to be Garland's last stand: on the second day,

rehearsing 'Sid's Ahead', Davis's second original composition, they had a disagreement and the pianist left the studio, to be replaced for that final tune by the leader himself. Of course, Davis could hardly play piano during the theme statements, or behind his own solo; but the temporary absence of the keyboard only enhanced the laconic, bluesy mood, while hindsight shows that his tentative, impressionistic note clusters, picked out behind the solos of Adderley and Coltrane, provided an explicit pre-echo of the distinctive touch of the next incumbent of the piano stool.

Miles Davis met Bill Evans through George Russell, who had employed the 29-year-old New Jersey pianist as a member of his Jazz Workshop band and had featured him in 1956 as the soloist in an extended work, 'All About Rosie' (another product of Gunther Schuller's Brandeis-sponsored commissioning spree). While fiercely proud of the Afro-American musical tradition, Davis was always prepared to defend the presence of white musicians in his band, and Evans's colour was no obstacle once Davis had decided this was the pianist he wanted. Evans had a good grasp of the essentials of modern jazz piano, including a lean sense of swing that owed something to the very straightforward Horace Silver, but he also had a harmonic sense that, while it may have been inspired by influences from Ravel to Lennie Tristano, had resulted in a completely personal approach. Evans's playing was gentle, but never weak;

romantic, but never sentimental; contemplative, but never passive. His special gift was to devise inner voicings that made his chords and clusters glow darkly from within, and he felt a great attraction to the new harmonic principles with which Davis was reorganising the music's internals. As Davis put it, he played 'underneath the rhythm', far less emphatically than Garland, but with such character that he changed the entire mood of the sextet's music.

Their first recorded collaboration came that May, at Columbia Studios, when the sextet recorded three standards – 'Love for Sale', 'On Green Dolphin Street' and 'Stella by Starlight' – and a single Davis original, 'Fran-Dance', which was dedicated to his current

His friendship with Gil Evans (right) provided the key relationship of Davis's career.

girlfriend, the dancer Frances Taylor. For this session there was another newcomer: Philly Joe Jones had gone again, replaced this time by Jimmy Cobb, an equally stylish but less assertive drummer who had made his reputation as a sensitive accompanist of singers. Davis had loved the sheer fire of Jones's playing, even when it threatened to overwhelm the other musicians, but the smoother ride provided by Cobb was more appropriate to the mood of the band with Evans at the piano.

Davis, Evans, Coltrane and Chambers, together with half a dozen other musicians, were convened a month later in another studio, under the baton of Michel Legrand, a French jazz pianist and arranger who was to become famous as a soundtrack composer. For this project, part of an album titled *Legrand Jazz*, the Frenchman had arranged four jazz standards: Fats Waller's 'Jitterbug Waltz', Monk's 'Round Midnight', Louis Armstrong and Jelly Roll Morton's 'Wild Man Blues' and John Lewis's 'Django'. Pleasant rather than profound, given a curious (and presumably intentional) kitsch edge by the prominent use of harp, flute and Eddie Costa's tremulous vibraharp, the pieces veered from first-class jazz soloing by Davis and Coltrane to passages that sounded as if they might have been scored as incidental music for *Monsieur Hulot's Holiday*.

The deficiencies of ordinary arrangers like Legrand were pointed up by Davis's next project, which reunited him with

Gil Evans for an orchestral recasting of George Gershwin's music for *Porgy and Bess*. The notion had occurred to Davis while watching Frances Taylor dancing in a New York production of the opera, and he had no trouble convincing Evans that here was a natural follow-up to *Miles Ahead*. Using similar resources, Evans devised a 12-song sequence of great coherence and integrity, enhancing the emotional contours of Gershwin's melodies with subtly imaginative touches. The textures were richer and more vibrant than ever, the risks taken with more confidence. The instrumental range, from tuba to piccolo, was exploited with enormous resource; the mood went from stationary tapestries of gorgeously wrought sound on 'Prayer' to the lean drive of 'Summertime' (set to Cobb's cool version of the clicking 'Philly lick' and buoyed up by a skeletal flute-and-brass riff, like a 'Milestones' writ large). On 'It Ain't Necessarily So' Davis delivered a flügelhorn solo of immaculate shape and trajectory, while Philly Joe was called back to turn 'Gone, Gone, Gone' into a concerto for drummer and jazz ensemble, launching Davis's solo and keeping it airborne with a combination of snare and bass-drum accents as audacious and sophisticated as anything of their kind.

Columbia released the album in a sleeve that showed how hard it was working to promote Davis's image. *Milestones* had the famous green shirt; now *Porgy and Bess* appeared with a cover photograph by Roy de Carava,

Cool and hot: by 1958, Davis and Dizzy Gillespie had come to represent the polarities of modern jazz.

cropped to show a trumpet on a player's lap, with a woman's hand reaching over her green-skirted thigh to touch the mouthpiece. The details included the trumpeter's soft white shirt and black skin, and the woman's plain gold bracelet on a light brown wrist. No faces. The focus blurred in a painterly way. Somewhere out of shot, outside the building, a new $8,000 Ferrari convertible. Miles and Frances, no doubt, in an image fit to hang on a gallery wall.

By the spring of 1959, though, the sextet was beginning to fly apart. Adderley and Coltrane, each hearing his own music, were planning to form their own bands. Evans was becoming depressed by criticism of his playing from those who thought that Davis shouldn't be employing white musicians. These centrifugal pressures began to exert their effect just as Davis was planning the group's masterpiece.

Kind of Blue, which was to become one of the key texts of jazz, was recorded over two days: 2 March and 22 April 1959. Carefully planned by Davis, with some assistance from Gil Evans, it was a summary of everything he had been working towards since the session of Christmas Eve 1954. Just to get the musicians together took some doing. Adderley was already working in a quintet with his brother, the cornetist Nat Adderley, and planning the deal with Riverside Records that would give him a series of hit albums throughout the early sixties. Coltrane had signed

with Atlantic Records and was weeks away from recording a quartet album, *Giant Steps*, that would begin to establish him as a guiding spirit of the avant garde. And Evans, after a short retirement at his brother's house in Louisiana, had returned to New York to organise the group that would revolutionise the piano-trio format. Davis had in fact already hired a new pianist, a 27-year-old Brooklynite of Jamaican extraction called Wynton Kelly, but since the new music had been designed around Evans's playing, Davis invited the previous incumbent back for the recording sessions.

It was Evans whose darkly luminous touch opened the album with the pensive introduction to 'So What', a call-and-response theme in which Chambers's solo phrases were answered by 'amen chords' from the horns. The latest of Davis's investigations of non-chordal playing, 'So What' slipped from scale to scale, each switch like the change in an automatic gearbox, raising and lowering the pressure. Davis's solo was one of his most beautiful constructions, gliding on the moving walkway of Cobb's cymbal beat. Coltrane and Adderley seemed to be given limitless space for their contrasting adventures, the tenor attacking the harmonic material head on and the alto skittering across its surface in a series of exhilarating slides and spurts.

The significance of *Kind of Blue* was that each of its five tunes seemed to invent its own idiom. Here there were no longer the conventional formats of the 12-bar blues or the 32-bar AABA standard tune. The content of a piece dictated its own formal structure. And the sum of the five pieces was a unique overall ambience. It was drenched in the feeling of the blues, but of a new kind of blues, elegant and eclectic, at once earthy and sophisticated.

There was an extraordinary slow blues ballad, 'Blue in Green', and a funky medium-tempo tune, 'Freddie Freeloader', for which Kelly, a more natural player of down-home blues than Evans, took over at the keyboard. But Evans's delicacy was crucial to the success of the two extended pieces, 'All Blues' and 'Flamenco Sketches', which provided the album's most strikingly intense moments. If 'Milestones' had been a highway ride, 'All Blues', a see-sawing tune in 6/8 time, seemed like a journey in an opium dream, circling around the D minor tonal centre as if in slow motion. Cobb's cymbal beat was like crystal; Chambers gave the beat a calm sway. In the coda, as Adderley and Coltrane breathed out the basic three-note vamp, Davis's muted trumpet stabbed little bursts of Morse: nine or ten Gs in a row, ricocheting off the saxophones as the music faded into infinity. 'Flamenco Sketches' was even more impressive, an almost tempo-less investigation of modes with a Moorish cast, a fine basis for creative improvisation.

Long afterwards, Davis suggested that he had not achieved everything he set

out to in *Kind of Blue*, but no such failure is audible to the outsider. It has a seamless unity of mood and performance, plus the extra quality that comes from working close to the edge. Davis had not written the tunes out in full; he merely presented the musicians with outline sketches that they first saw when they arrived at the sessions. No wonder every note still sounds morning fresh.

In recent years there have been suggestions that the album's narcotic atmosphere was the result of a technical accident – perhaps caused by the tapes being accidentally slowed down at some point during the recording or production process. Certainly the pulse of the music is abnormally slow: *Kind of Blue* unfolds with an exaggerated tranquillity that seems to have no relationship with the speed of the outside world. But a comparison between the pitch of these tunes and versions subsequently recorded in concert shows that the keys are those in which Davis continued to play them. This both suggests that *Kind of Blue* is an accurate transcription and demonstrates again what an extraordinary spell these men were under on those two days in the spring of 1959.

After the sessions, Evans left for good. Adderley stayed on for a while and Coltrane came back when Davis took the band into Birdland towards the end of August. One night during the engagement Davis was seeing an acquaintance, a white woman, into a car

on the sidewalk outside the club when a policeman challenged him, telling him to move on. I'm working here, Davis told him, pointing to his name in lights. Move on, said the cop. Davis wouldn't retreat, and the policeman started to handcuff him. What happened next remains unclear, but a second policeman materialised and hit Davis on the head with a nightstick. The trumpeter fell, bleeding from his wound. Passers-by and people from inside the club gathered as Davis was carted off to the 54th Precinct, where he was charged with resisting arrest and assaulting a police officer, and duly locked up.

The following morning the story was on the front pages of the New York papers, dramatised by a picture of Davis being led away, bleeding profusely from the head. The fuss got him released, but it was two months before the court ruled that he had been wrongfully arrested. Coming at a time of gathering acclaim and personal stability, the experience reawakened his bitter feelings about American racism. Everything he ever said or did showed that Davis felt no animosity towards white people as individuals; but he could hardly be blamed if, after the Birdland incident, he felt that his father had been right all along, and that blacks could expect no justice from the white world.

Now Davis was exhausted, drained by the arrest and by the intensity of running the sextet. Before he could take a break, though, there was one other project to undertake with Gil Evans; their version

of Joaquín Rodrigo's popular 'Concierto de Aranjuez', a work for guitar and orchestra which Evans set about recasting for their own resources. Davis had heard the concerto on record at the house of the bassist Joe Mondragon in California, and had fallen in love with the power of the melodies and with the atmosphere created by the Spanish modes. He and Evans cast around for other complementary material to fill the album, which was to be called *Sketches of Spain*.

The more self-consciously rigorous critics regarded *Sketches of Spain* as fatally compromised by its borrowings from the European classical tradition, too far from the Afro-American heritage for comfort or credibility. Davis, though, was aware of the relationship between Spain and Africa, and felt that he was merely investigating another aspect of his own roots. But the shimmering textures and driving flamenco-derived rhythms needed no spurious justification: his audience responded straight away to the ecstasy and pain on display in Davis's trumpet throughout pieces like 'Saeta', the breathtaking recreation of a saint's day parade through a village street, and 'Solea', a magnificent essay in flamenco materials which produced one of Davis's most spellbindingly dramatic solos. No, the Miles Davis/Gil Evans 'Concierto de Aranjuez' was not 'Bags' Groove' or · 'Straight, No Chaser'. It was something else: something new, something of its own kind, something never to be repeated.

7

1960-67

the second
quintet

the second quintet

Left: London, 1967.
The second quintet,
with Wayne Shorter,
rewrote the rule
book.

Right: Copenhagen,
1964. The youthful
fire of the new line-
up reinvigorated
Davis's own playing,
which brooded less
and burned more.

everything was going right. Davis's music, with both the small group and the orchestra, had reached a pinnacle. His own playing, in solos like those on 'So What' and 'Solea', was at a phenomenal pitch of invention. He seemed to have mastered the combination that musicians and sportsmen, people who perform in real time, without the possibility of correcting errors or retouching flaws, strive for: the quality best described as relaxed intensity. People were flocking to see him. But, just as his achievements and his celebrity were running in tandem, so the disintegration began.

Adderley had gone; Evans was out; Coltrane wanted to be on his way. These were the key creative components of the sextet. Kelly, Chambers and Cobb, the finest of craftsmen, were the supporting cast. It was one aspect of Davis's genius that he could identify the innovators before anyone else, and then bind them together into an extraordinary collective endeavour. Not for ever, though: the elements were too volatile to be held in combination, and Davis's problem was what to do next.

Cannonball was already launched towards solo stardom. In October 1959 he and his new quintet had been recorded at the Jazz Workshop in San Francisco. From the resulting album, a tune called 'This Here' by their pianist, Bobby Timmons, became a hit, adding impetus to the growing fashion for a new kind of modern music – 'soul jazz', which rejected the cerebral investigations of bebop and cool jazz, preferring a heavy backbeat and devices borrowed from gospel music. Evans, on the other hand, had pursued his instinct for delicacy, obliqueness and introspection. He recruited a young virtuoso of the double bass, 23-year-old Scott LaFaro, and a gifted and original drummer, Paul Motian. *Portrait in Jazz*, their first album together, demonstrated that the days of piano-with-rhythm-accompaniment were gone: all three musicians could improvise simultaneously, bearing an equal responsibility.

Coltrane was on the verge of even greater discoveries. In April and May 1959 he recorded the material for *Giant Steps*, which showed that he was finding

his way towards a new level of playing and composing, making something new of the lessons he'd learnt with Monk and Davis. In the early months of 1960 he was planning the line-up of a permanent quartet to take his investigations even further, and had identified the pianist McCoy Tyner and the drummer Elvin Jones as two outstanding prospects. In fact, Coltrane was to display the gift that Davis had for taking musicians whose previous work had been good but not conspicuous and providing the context in which true originality could bud and blossom.

Now Davis talked him into making one last European tour before embarking on his own adventures. The surviving evidence, mostly from concerts recorded in Stockholm, shows the quintet performing with imperious control. The contrast between Davis's poised purity and Coltrane's clamorous roughness was even more marked now that Coltrane was letting fly with his famous 'sheets of sound' and his pioneering explorations of multiphonics – an attempt to split notes into two distinct pitches which, in its early days, produced a decidedly unlovely sound. It was during this tour that Davis gave Coltrane a soprano saxophone, an instrument which had

Backstage in Stockholm with his first wife, the dancer Frances Taylor.

fallen into almost total disuse. But the gift was to echo around the world once Coltrane had made it a feature of his work with his new group; by the mid-sixties, no young tenor saxophonist could afford to be seen without a small, straight horn in his armoury. Behind Coltrane and Davis on the European dates, the Kelly–Chambers–Cobb rhythm section supplied the ideal gear-ratio for every tempo and gradient. Davis had said that Kelly's special virtue was his ability to provide the group with both the funky blues touch of Red Garland and the harmonic delicacy of Bill Evans, but this was something of a back-handed compliment. Kelly would never be an innovator, but he was more than a mere copyist. Until his untimely death in 1971 his playing was marked by

a sunny, springy lyricism that may not have been the stuff of tragic heroes but made him, in a small way, a genuine original.

When they got back to New York, Coltrane was quickly away to rehearse for the opening at the Jazz Gallery with his own quartet, the beginning of an odyssey that would have as much impact as *Kind of Blue*. For Davis, the problem of finding another front-line voice of equal weight proved a tough one to resolve. Several tenor-players came and went. Jimmy Heath, a Philadelphian who had been known in the late forties – when he often played alto – as 'Little Bird', and who had played on Davis's Blue Note dates in 1953, was the first to replace Coltrane, but parole after a prison spell following a heroin

The final days of the old quintet: with Coltrane in Stockholm, during the last European tour.

conviction restricted his movements to within a 60-mile radius of his home town, which wasn't much good to Davis. Sonny Stitt, also an experienced Parker disciple, was the next, and travelled to Europe with Davis for another tour in the autumn of 1960, but his conventional bebop sensibility removed a dimension from the group's music. Although Stitt was a musician of considerable gifts, his vision extended no further than the frontiers defined by Parker: as far as he was concerned, the more chords the better, and *Milestones* and *Kind of Blue* might never have happened.

Hank Mobley, who replaced Stitt at the beginning of 1961, lasted a little longer: long enough to be heard on some of the sessions that made up a studio album titled *Someday My Prince Will Come*, and to be featured on a pair of albums recorded live at the Blackhawk club in San Francisco. Mobley, 30 years old when he joined Davis, had been born in Georgia and raised in New Jersey. An early member of the two key groups of the hard-bop movement, Art Blakey's Jazz Messengers and the Horace Silver Quintet, he was also a favourite of Blue Note's Alfred Lion and Francis Wolff, who recorded a long series of albums under his name. Mobley wasn't Coltrane, but he wasn't Heath or Stitt either. He had a small, slightly husky sound, a disinclination to play a lot of notes, and a wonderfully nonchalant rhythmic sense. Like Kelly, he could lay claim to the status of a minor original. The tenorist and the pianist also shared a natural affinity for the blues, glimpsed during

Mobley's solo on 'Walkin' ' at the Blackhawk, when the two of them fell naturally into a passage of pure rhythm and blues.

On 19 May 1961, the same band appeared on a larger stage – at Carnegie Hall in New York, along with a 21-piece orchestra directed by Gil Evans. Their only concert appearance together, it included the 'Concierto de Aranjuez' and some of the material from *Miles Ahead* – 'Lament', 'New Rhumba' and 'The Meaning of the Blues' – plus a set by the quintet. Critics who had not heard Davis

in person for a while were enthralled by the new fire and drive in his playing. Some felt he had been needled into playing his very best by an unexpected event: an African nationalist sit-down demonstration on stage, led by his old friend Max Roach, in protest against the precise activities of the medical-aid-for-Africa charity on whose behalf Davis was appearing. The next morning, the New York papers contained ecstatic descriptions of an event that quickly passed into legend. Columbia Records, who had recorded the concert, swiftly edited and released it, with excerpts from the reviews on the back of the sleeve.

Although they were full of fine, aggressive modern jazz, however, the Blackhawk and Carnegie Hall albums weren't making history in the sense of defining new directions. In fact, having abandoned the intensity of the *Kind of Blue* era, the music seemed to be moving backwards, towards a sophisticated form of hard bop. But now the sixties were starting, and everything was in play, up for grabs. It was the most inconvenient of moments for Davis to run out of ideas, even temporarily. And while he was standing still, he was being overtaken not only by his former sidemen but by a host of new arrivals – principally the Texan alto saxophonist Ornette Coleman, whose young quartet, bearing the standard of 'free jazz', was attracting opinion-formers and scene-makers to the Five Spot every night. Whereas once his elders had gone to check him out, now

With Stan Getz and Frances Taylor in Stockholm.

Davis went to have a look at Coleman and his equally controversial partner, the trumpeter Don Cherry. Davis couldn't see beyond Coleman's plastic alto and Cherry's Pakistani pocket trumpet. Afterwards he was publicly critical of them, as he was to be of other musicians, such as the saxophonist Eric Dolphy and the pianist Cecil Taylor, who made up the advance guard of the movement that became known as the 'new thing'.

This sourly disparaging tone became a characteristic of Davis's middle years, and did him no honour. His fierce powers of discrimination were not in doubt, but his inability to have a good word for the likes of Coleman and Taylor seemed as much to do with professional rivalry as with aesthetic judgement. He didn't like being outpaced, he hated the suggestion that he might no longer be in the vanguard, and instead of keeping his own counsel he reacted badly. 'That's some sad shit, man,' he told the critic Leonard Feather while listening to a Taylor piece for *Down Beat* magazine's Blindfold Test. 'He's a sad shit,' was his verdict on Dolphy. A rich man, newly married to Frances Taylor, with a big house on the Upper West Side and a Ferrari in his garage, he surely had nothing to fear from struggling fellow musicians who could hardly have been doing anything less likely to damage him commercially. But where he could have afforded to show generosity, he used his position and celebrity to damage them. Maybe he simply had the good of the music at heart and genuinely perceived

danger in the wholesale rush to publicise the avant garde. He wasn't obliged to be nice about them just for the sake of politeness. But if his own artistic record at the time was pretty well impeccable, some of the more dubious achievements in his future were to cast serious doubt on his right to criticise men like Coleman and Cherry, whose sincerity was unquestionable. Of all the leaders of the avant-garde movement, only Coltrane, his former sideman, was exempt from withering censure; for how could Davis criticise Coltrane without implicitly casting a shadow on his own judgement?

Standing still was not his natural mode, though, and it made him itchy. Working out in his own basement gym and checking the progress of his stocks in the *Wall Street Journal* made a nice reward, as did the many plaques that came in from magazine polls around the world, but he wasn't ready for retirement from the creative arena. Waiting for fresh inspiration to strike, he shuffled the pack: out went Mobley, back came Rollins and J.J. Johnson, then Jimmy Heath, followed by three Memphis musicians – the altoist Frank Strozier, tenorist George Coleman and pianist Harold Mabern.

There wasn't much to show for 1962. At a strange recording date with singer Bob Dorough, a white hipster, Davis found himself playing for the first time with Wayne Shorter, a quiet 29-year-old tenorist from Newark, New Jersey, who was the current musical director of Art

Heading for the stage in Stockholm, with Jimmy Cobb and Wynton Kelly.

Blakey's Jazz Messengers and who had actually called Davis to offer himself as Coltrane's replacement a couple of years earlier. And Gil Evans, a notoriously slow worker, had produced five new arrangements which, augmented by a single quintet track, were turned into an album called *Quiet Nights* – lovely music but, at less than 27 minutes in total, not a commodity the critics felt they could recommend wholeheartedly. In fact, Davis and Evans regarded the project as incomplete and were angry when it was released. But their view of Brazilian music, as displayed in Jobim's 'Corcovado' and Pinto Goncalves's 'Aos Pes Da Cruz', was as sensitive as their vision of Spain, although if it was an attempt to jump on the rolling bossa nova bandwagon then it lacked the sort of commercial conviction Columbia might have been hoping for.

More significantly, Davis's father died during the year, having been ill ever since his car was hit by a train on an unguarded level crossing a couple of years earlier. According to his son, the funeral, in Lincoln High School gymnasium, was one of the biggest ever held for a black man in East St Louis. The trumpeter, who knew his father had given him strength and a pride in his race, felt the loss deeply. It seemed like a good time to move on.

At the beginning of 1963, the rhythm section announced its desire to go off on its own. Hardly any of the new horn players sounded right. But Davis remembered the time Chambers had

Previous pages: Stockholm, autumn 1960.

Sonny Stitt (right) took Coltrane's place on the second European tour of 1960.

With Wynton Kelly
and the impresario
Norman Granz.

The rhythm section:
Jimmy Cobb, Wynton
Kelly and Paul
Chambers raised the
art of
accompaniment to a
new level of discreet
sensitivity.

London, 1960: backstage at the Gaumont Cinema, Hammersmith.

Above: On tour: at a
Swedish airport with
Jimmy Cobb, 1960.

Opposite: On stage at
Carnegie Hall, in the
great concert with
the quintet and the
Gil Evans Orchestra
on 19 May 1961.

introduced him to another young Detroit bassist, Ron Carter, a 25-year-old former student of the Eastman School of Music, and went to hear him with the Art Farmer/Jim Hall Quartet. Davis found a player with a finely shaped tone and a supple, athletic delivery. Carter wanted to join Davis, but decently insisted that Farmer must give his consent. Reluctantly, perhaps mindful (in his calm, gentlemanly way) of the artistic debt he owed Davis, as well as of the greater career opportunity Davis represented, Farmer gave Carter his blessing. Straight away, Carter and Davis went out to California. There, with the drummer Frank Butler, whose attacking style and heroin problems made him the West Coast's equivalent of Philly Joe Jones, and the expatriate English pianist Victor Feldman, they recorded three tracks for an album that was to be named after one of Feldman's compositions: *Seven Steps to Heaven.*

Davis offered Feldman a regular berth in the group, but the Englishman was making too much money in the Hollywood studios to contemplate the rigours of life on the road.

Back in New York, Davis went head-hunting again. For the drum stool, he had one name in mind. Tony Williams was only 17, but he'd been the talk of the Manhattan scene ever since his arrival from Boston the previous year to join Jackie McLean's quintet. The son of a tenor saxophonist, Williams had grown up amidst Boston's thriving jazz community and had become an authentic virtuoso by the time he reached his mid-teens. In addition to superlative technique, he also possessed an in-built unwillingness to settle for the conventions. This wasn't the hare-brained iconoclasm of the standard-issue revolutionary: Williams was one of those who believed that the way to make real progress was to learn the rules before you started breaking them.

To complete the rhythm section, Davis called up another prodigy, Herbie Hancock, who had played Mozart's D major piano concerto with the Cleveland Symphony Orchestra at the age of 11 and now, at 22, had a Blue Note recording deal and a first hit record, the funky and much-covered 'Watermelon Man', to his name.

The three young men were invited to Davis's house, where they played together for the first time. Not wanting to intimidate them, the trumpeter stayed out of their way for the first couple of days, listening to them over an internal speaker system. Eventually he'd heard enough, and joined them. But perhaps the decision to leave them alone was the crucial move: those first hours together, free from pressure, may have begun the bonding process that turned them into one of the most remarkable rhythm sections in all of jazz.

A few days later, with George Coleman on tenor, they were all in the studio together, recording enough tracks to complete *Seven Steps to Heaven*. Then they were on the road. For the next 12 months, with Davis's encouragement, Hancock, Carter and Williams worked together to take the evolution of the rhythm section to a new level — to bypass, as some saw it, the 'free jazz' of Coleman, Taylor, Dolphy and the tenor saxophonist Albert Ayler, simply by doing everything better than it had been done before. Their phenomenal skills, extreme intelligence and youthful arrogance allowed them to take everything further: they could play faster than anyone, or — with equally breathtaking effect — slower. They could each shoot off at oblique angles, trusted by the others to find their own way back to the centre of the tune. In fact they could all do this simultaneously, leading to the terrifying and exhilarating sensation of watching three trapeze artists in mid-air without a safety net. Carter could leave immense, vertigo-inducing holes in the bass line; Hancock could take the harmony to its outer limit; Williams could break the time up into abstruse sub-divisions that nudged and sometimes kicked the soloist into a fresh perspective.

Davis loved the new drummer above all. A cocky little fellow, Williams was passionate about music. He wanted to know about everything: melody and harmony as well as rhythm. As far as percussion technique went, at 17 he literally had nothing further to learn; already he knew more than Kenny Clarke or Max Roach or Art Blakey or Philly Joe Jones. So his mind was free to concentrate on other aspects of music – an opportunity he never failed to exploit, and which was to make him the most musicianly of drummers. But you didn't play with Tony Williams if you weren't in his league. 'Man,' Davis was to say fondly, 'to play with Tony Williams you had to be real alert and pay attention to everything he did, or he'd lose you in a second, and you'd just be out of tempo and time and sound real bad.' Williams, he added, was the centre that the group's sound revolved around. 'I loved him like a son.' Williams's own enthusiasm for the music of Ornette Coleman and other members of the avant garde, quickly evident in the albums (titled *Life Time* and *Spring*) the drummer was to make for Blue Note in the mid-sixties, also forced Davis to reassess his attitudes, at least in private.

The odd man out was George Coleman, a musician of a slightly earlier generation. Although only 28 years old, he had grown up in Memphis, Tennessee, in the middle of the bebop tradition, and had turned himself into a master player of what post-bop musicians called 'time-and-changes'. Coleman had as much technique, in relation to his own instrument, as any of the Davis quintet, but he was not by temperament an explorer, and some of the band, Williams in particular, felt that he was holding them back. Events were to prove the drummer right, but the justification for Coleman's self-belief was to come in the 1980s, when he became recognised as one of the most gifted exponents of the tenor saxophone.

He was still in the quintet on 12 February 1964, when they appeared in New York, at Lincoln Centre's Philharmonic Hall, in a benefit for voter registration in Louisiana and Mississippi run by the National Association for the Advancement of Coloured People and the Student Non-violent Co-ordinating Committee, two bodies prominent in the civil rights struggle. Whatever the inspiration, the quintet was in remarkable form during a concert that was recorded and issued by Columbia in two volumes, *My Funny Valentine* and *'Four' and More*. In their way, these albums were as astonishing and influential as *Milestones* and *Kind of Blue*. But whereas the innovations of those albums had been largely formal, here the revelation was the method of collective improvisation. There was still a soloist, but the 'accompanists' took a far freer role, liberated to comment from whatever angle they chose. In 'All of You', for instance, Williams and

Ladies' man: Davis in Copenhagen in the early sixties.

more tenorists – Sam Rivers, an older Bostonian who came enthusiastically recommended by Williams, and Rocky Boyd. Rivers went along on a tour of Japan which yielded another excellent live album, but he wasn't what Davis was looking for. Davis wanted Wayne Shorter, but he had to wait until Shorter left the Jazz Messengers. When Davis heard the news that Shorter had handed in his resignation, he told Hancock, Carter and Williams to call the tenorist and urge him to accept the invitation.

Wayne Shorter is one of those great jazz musicians who seem curiously uneasy with the role, giving the impression of being set apart from their fellows by some strange angle in the formation of their characters. Thelonious Monk and Sonny Rollins were others: blessed with absolute mastery of their craft, and with an utterly unique vision, they nevertheless showed a reluctance to commit themselves which suggested that their gifts might have been applied with equal or greater success to some other field – Monk, for instance, who might have been happier with some more private art, could have become the one beat poet to do work of lasting value, while Rollins's analytical imagination and sense of structure might have turned him into a great architect, had he not been born into a community of jazz musicians in New York City. In Wayne Shorter's case, a diffident and abstracted manner, suggestive perhaps of a professor of literature, formed a powerfully original

Hancock could stop playing altogether, leaving Davis alone with Carter; the tempo could be halved, doubled, redoubled, abandoned altogether; the chord sequence could be extended, compressed, suspended, ignored. Before this, drummers had always pedalled their hi-hat cymbals on the backbeat – the second and fourth beats of the bar; but if Williams felt like mashing it down on 1 and 3, that was what he did – and made it sound exquisitely hip.

When Coleman finally left in the middle of 1964, Davis briefly tried two musical personality, which found in the Miles Davis Quintet the perfect vehicle for its expression.

'Tony was the fire, the creative spark,' Davis said. 'Wayne was the idea person. Ron and Herbie were the anchors.' To say they upped the ante is understating it. They simply changed the game. To enjoy it, though, you didn't need a degree in whatever form of higher rhythmic and harmonic calculus they'd studied. The emotion of the music was never lost beneath the technicalities. In fact the music was more emotional than ever, partly because the youth of the players made them more aggressive, which brought the extrovert out of Miles Davis. On the quintet's first studio albums, *ESP* and *Miles Smiles*, he played with the brio of an 18-year-old, matching the ferocious energy levels of his new colleagues. Gone was the solitary, brooding presence dominating his surroundings; he was a partner in this endeavour, relishing the input of the younger men, and the way they were inventing a secret language together. The themes were cryptic and unsentimental; in this, at least, they must have reminded Davis of the nights at Minton's, when the inventors of bebop struggled to hold on to their private language and to keep the squares at bay. The quintet had the same sense of superiority, and with equal justification.

Everybody in the band contributed themes (Davis himself was inspired to start writing again, after several barren years), and from the writing the new

forms began to emerge, bearing the imprint of young men's interests. In the mid-sixties, no one could miss hearing the Beatles and Motown; even jazz musicians, dismissive over the previous decades of everyone from Paul Whiteman to Elvis Presley, acknowledged their significance. Davis himself loved soul music: James Brown, the Temptations, Dionne Warwick. He was also jealous of their popularity, of their ability to claim the attention of

Davis with Frances in London, 1960.

Copenhagen, 1964:
bassist Ron Carter
was the linch-pin of
the new quintet, a
virtuoso who struck
up a brilliant rapport
with his colleagues.

Above & right: Berlin Philharmonie, 25 September 1964: they were simply untouchable. Miles Davis, Wayne Shorter, Herbie Hancock, Ron Carter and Tony Williams could think things that had never been thought before, and then do them.

Left & below: Berlin
again: Davis's
partnership with
Wayne Shorter
produced a laconic,
dry-toned blend.

large numbers of young people. So Tony Williams's 'Eighty-one', on *ESP*, was the first piece by any Davis band to abandon the conventional 4/4 handed down from bebop in favour of the straight 8/8 of most pop music. So cunning was Williams in his writing and his playing that he could transfer the flexibility of the triplet-based 4/4 to the ostensibly more restrictive 8/8; in fact he could float backwards and forwards between them, or superimpose one upon the other at will. Others, with less intellectual or technical ability, would not be so creative when faced by the same material, but it would be unfair to blame Williams, or Davis, for the countless thousands of man-years wasted in the development of jazz-rock (later known as fusion music) over the next quarter-century.

Even the nature of improvising changed in this band. As they progressed through their four years together, the solos and the compositions became more carefully entwined. Sometimes the horns would not solo at all, instead simply stating a written theme; the element of improvisation would come from what the rhythm section was doing. Or perhaps it would be in the phrasing, and there would be no overt improvising at all. At its best, particularly in the albums called *Sorcerer* and *Nefertiti*, the quintet could make the listener forget that there was any difference between composing and improvising.

Herbie Hancock gave a vivid description of their method when he explained the origins of Shorter's tune 'Nefertiti', in which the only improvising seemed to be done by the

Jazz Expo, London, 1967: the suit was still there, but the mind was turning elsewhere.

drummer: 'We were in the recording studio, and Wayne brought it in. We were trying to learn the song. Miles gave me a part. He was trying to play the melody and Wayne was sort of following behind. Wayne could have just played it, but he wanted to see Miles's interpretation of it. The rhythm section was working on it and we would play it over and over again while they'd play the melody. Finally I said to Miles, "Listen, the melody is so beautiful, how would it be if the horns basically played the melody and the rhythm section actually evolved?" He said, "Okay." That's what we did. Any kind of idea like that, Miles was more than willing to open up to.'

They were like a group of Zen masters. While no one else even suspected the existence of a question, they had found the answer. And, having heard the answer, the rest of the world then had to go back and figure out the question. They could never be caught. When the five of them were together, nobody else had a chance.

When Davis and Shorter played together, sometimes it was hard to tell where composition ended and improvisation began.

115

8

on the

corner

the beat was changing. Davis's mother had died in St Louis, affecting him so badly that he couldn't attend the funeral. His marriage to Frances was breaking down, heading for divorce. Then John Coltrane died, his liver eaten away, his musical odyssey unfinished. The quintet toured, recorded, rested, toured again. But Davis's ears were open to what was happening among a younger audience: open to Jimi Hendrix and Cream, to James Brown and Sly and the Family Stone, and to Norman Whitfield's epic psych-soul productions with the Temptations. Some of it he heard through a young singer called Betty Mabry, with whom he had begun a relationship. Suddenly 'Dance to the Music' and 'Cloud Nine' sounded fresher and more interesting than 'On Green Dolphin Street' or 'Round Midnight'; the quintet played concert halls when it went on tour abroad, but in the US it mostly played jazz clubs, and Davis was getting tired of the stereotyped response he found there. He wanted to play to people who hadn't heard it all before.

In December 1967 he and the quintet went into the studios, accompanied by Gil Evans and a young guitarist, Joe Beck. For the first time, Herbie Hancock played an electric piano with the band. The sonorities were new, but the reorganisation of the music was even more significant. Beck, Hancock and Carter started to play riffs together, like the rhythm section on a soul record. They could either play in a tight unison, like the house rhythm section on the Stax records by Otis Redding and Sam and Dave, or they could dovetail their individual parts, like James Brown's musicians. Either way, it was a much more arranged way of playing, and it had evolved naturally from the quintet's experiments on records like *Nefertiti* and *Sorcerer*.

Davis wasn't entirely happy with the Beck session, and in the early weeks of 1968 he went back into the studio with a different guitarist. George Benson was a brilliant 24-year-old who had been playing with name bands since his teens; years after his brief association with Davis he would parlay a pleasant singing voice into a career that made him a million-selling latter-day equivalent of

By 1969, the suits and ties had gone for good. Now the silks and satins brought him into line with the new generation of rock stars.

By the time Davis
appeared at Newport
in 1968, the quintet
was exploring
electronic textures
and rock rhythms.

of all those 78s carrying the legend 'Soloist with rhythm accompaniment' on the label), now the density of the music inverted itself. Thanks to James Brown, the rhythm section had started to dominate. Thanks to Brown, again, and also to John Coltrane and Gil Evans, the time-frame of the music had also started to change. Music was getting longer, and a mid-sixties interest in Indian music (felt by everyone from Coltrane to the Beatles) led to a reduction in harmonic movement in favour of pieces based on only one or two chords. This was picked up by the early psychedelic groups in San Francisco: the Grateful Dead's Jerry Garcia and Bob Weir jammed for hours on a single chord, as did Jefferson Airplane's Jorma Kaukonen and Jack Casady. Davis, who (with Evans) had been responsible for the first harmonic reductions in the *Milestones* era, found this idea highly congenial. Rhythm had always been important to him, and the chance to reorganise the whole rhythmic basis of his music, divesting it of the last traces of the bebop heritage, seemed like the right opportunity in a changing time.

It had another benefit, too. Paradoxically, the busier and denser the rhythm section became, the more the trumpet solos would be thrown into relief. He could let the music burn on, choosing his moment to enter; pausing when he wished; ending whenever he felt like it. There would be no arbitrary signposts – chord changes or chorus lengths – to restrict his range of choice.

As far as the public was concerned,

Nat 'King' Cole. Back in 1968, Davis found him a funkier player than Beck. 'I wanted to hear the bass line a little stronger,' the trumpeter said. In fact he wanted a rooted, repetitive bass line rather than the walking 4/4 of bop and post-bop music, and he wanted the rhythm section as a whole to occupy more space in the music.

This represented one of the most crucial changes in post-war music. Whereas the voice or the soloist had previously been the centre of the aural focus, dominating the background (think

At the Isle of Wight
Pop Festival in 1970,
Davis played to more
than half a million
rock fans.

the first visible sign of this development was an album called *Miles in the Sky*, released at about the time of Davis's marriage to Betty Mabry, in the autumn of 1968. The cover suggested that something was up: a painting of concentric circles in shades ranging from hot orange to deep purple, it looked like the sort of thing that one of the Haight-Ashbury bands might go for. The album contained four long pieces, with Hancock's electric piano heavily featured over the tongue-and-groove 8/8 rhythms laid down by Tony Williams and Ron Carter. One track, 'Paraphernalia', featured Benson's guitar, functioning in the way rhythm guitarists worked on records by James Brown or Otis Redding, flicking out little figures that were part of the structure, rather than mere decoration. And the busier the rhythm section became, the sparer were the horns – increasing the music's sense of drama.

The next album, *Filles de Kilimanjaro*, had Betty Mabry's face on the cover and evidence of the disintegration of the great quintet inside. On two of the five tunes, there were new names: pianist Chick Corea and bassist Dave Holland. Hancock had moved on: his Blue Note recordings had been doing well, particularly 'Watermelon Man' and 'Maiden Voyage', and he planned to launch his own band. As for Carter, the great virtuoso of the bass violin simply wasn't interested in the electric bass guitar, which Davis now reckoned to be essential to any music he might want to

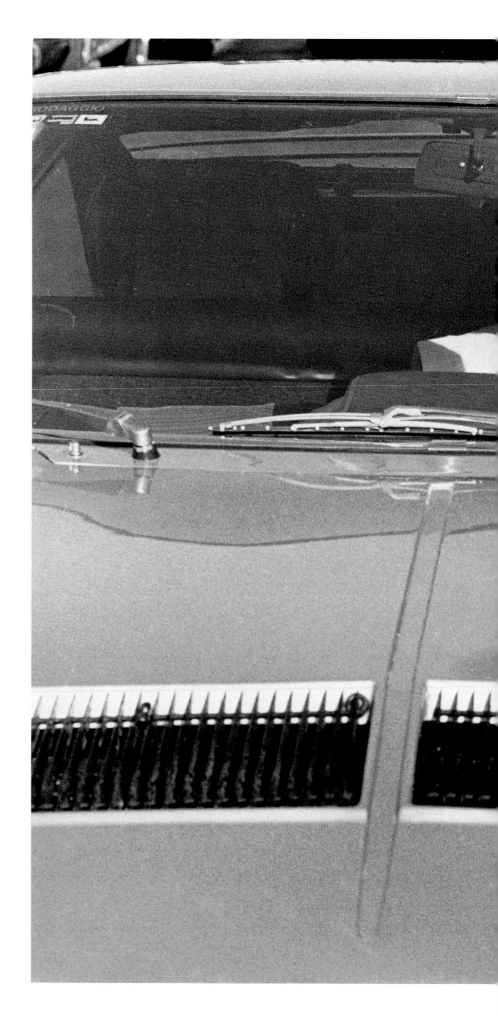

play in the future. Davis had heard Holland, a 21-year-old Englishman, playing in a London jazz club. The trumpeter's infallible ear was working well: he invited Holland to New York and the new man went on to become one of the most creative and admired bassists of the seventies and eighties. Corea, aged 27, had worked in New York with various Latin bands, including that of the percussionist Mongo Santamaria, and with Stan Getz; he came in on the recommendation of Tony Williams, a fellow Bostonian. The year Corea joined Davis he also recorded a superlative album of acoustic piano-trio jazz, under the title *Now He Sings, Now He Sobs*. But on *Filles de Kilimanjaro*, the

presence of two newcomers was hardly apparent: the music seemed to be evolving under its own momentum, gathering confidence in its new direction. The pretty 'Mademoiselle Mabry' had all the delicacy of the old music, while the atmospheric title track showed off the timeless, suspended quality of the new.

But it was with his next album that Miles Davis's new direction really made itself felt. *In a Silent Way*, released in the autumn of 1969, reasserted his claims to leadership. Richer and more complex than its immediate predecessors, it made use of three keyboard-players: Hancock, Corea and the Viennese expatriate Josef Zawinul,

Previous pages: He loved fast Italian cars. This was his silver Lamborghini Miura.

Opposite: Isle of Wight: on a beautiful late-summer afternoon, Davis followed Tiny Tim and Joni Mitchell, ending his set in the twilight.

Below: In transition: at Hammersmith Odeon in 1969 with Wayne Shorter and Dave Holland.

**'I can put together a
better band than Jimi
Hendrix,' he said.**

Opposite: **The
contender: this was
how he presented
himself to the
readers of *Rolling
Stone* at the time of
*Bitches Brew.***

whose use of electric piano on the
Cannonball Adderley Quintet's hit tune
'Mercy, Mercy, Mercy' in 1967 had
inspired Davis to persuade Hancock to
take it up. There was also another
Englishman in the line-up. John
McLaughlin's guitar had been one of the
most compelling voices on the London
scene in the mid-sixties. Introduced to
Davis and Tony Williams by Holland,
McLaughlin had arrived in New York to
join the band Williams was about to

leave Davis to form. But before they
could get under way, Davis called them
both in to play on the two long tracks
that made up *In a Silent Way.*

The secrets of the album's success
were the spare loveliness of its textures,
with Shorter's sweet-toned soprano
saxophone piping above the shimmer of
the massed keyboards and the subtle
ticking of Williams's rimshots, and its
calm, unhurried pacing. With two
extended tracks, both staying inside a

narrow dynamic and emotional range, this was the answer to a hippie's prayer: the perfect album to get stoned to. And lest there be doubt as to the identity of its author, the legend 'Directions in music by Miles Davis' made its first appearance on the cover.

His efforts to contact a new audience weren't restricted to the records. Cutting back on engagements at old-fashioned jazz clubs, now he was aiming for the rock audience in its own habitat: at Bill Graham's Fillmore West in San Francisco and Fillmore East in New York he appeared on bills alongside such stars of the Woodstock generation as

Santana, the Grateful Dead, Laura Nyro and the Steve Miller Band. He was wearing satins, velvets and silks. There were no breaks in the concert performances; the last vestiges of the Broadway ballad had vanished.

And in 1970 he released the recording that was to bring him closest to that audience. Like Hendrix's *Electric Ladyland*, the Beatles' white album and Cream's *Wheels of Fire*, Davis's *Bitches Brew* was a double album: a fashionable format which seemed to suggest that the artist had so much to say that it could not be contained within a single disc. In fact most double albums are an excuse

for the artist to avoid the responsibility for editing the work properly. This was not true of *Bitches Brew* for the simple reason that Davis no longer believed in editing. His views on the structure of music had now taken up a position completely opposed to traditional Western values. On *Bitches Brew*, Miles Davis's music seemed to have no beginnings and no ends. It began when the tape started and ended when it ran out. There were solos, but they no longer seemed to be subject to the old informal laws of statement, variation and conclusion; some of Davis's own playing had as much intrinsic beauty as anything he played on *Porgy and Bess* or *Sketches of Spain*, but the context was utterly different. Beneath the trumpet and the saxophone, a huge augmented rhythm section – McLaughlin, Corea and Holland joined by three new drummers, Jack DeJohnette, Lennie White and Don Alias, and another bass guitarist, the session-man Harvey Brooks – created an undergrowth seething with half-hidden life, around which prowled the mysterious bass clarinet of Bennie Maupin.

Favourable reviews in rock papers like *Rolling Stone* gave the album a terrific reputation, but the rock audience's opinion of Miles Davis never really lived up to his own aspirations. When he played the Isle of Wight Pop Festival in the autumn of 1970, on a bill with Hendrix, Sly, the Who, Chicago, Joni Mitchell, Tiny Tim, Leonard Cohen, the Doors and many others, he came face to face with roughly half a million members of the new rock tribe. Late in the afternoon of a beautiful day, he played with great clarity and lyricism, fronting a band that included Corea, Holland and DeJohnette plus a second pianist, Keith Jarrett (DeJohnette's erstwhile colleague in the popular Charles Lloyd Quartet), the alto saxophonist Gary Bartz and a Brazilian percussionist, Airto Moreira, who came equipped with a steamer trunk full of guiros, cabassas, berimbaus, asses' jawbones and other percussive

exotica. Bartz's presence could be explained by the departure of Wayne Shorter to join Joe Zawinul in founding a new quartet, called Weather Report. The Isle of Wight audience applauded politely, but this new rock-inflected jazz didn't move them to ecstasy. They knew Davis was important, and acknowledged the validity of his reputation, but his music didn't come close to their hearts in the way that Hendrix's guitar or Jim Morrison's voice did. Davis wanted the acceptance of the rock crowd, but even in this form his music was too rarified to stand a chance.

He recorded heavily all the way through 1970, bringing young musicians into the studios to help him realise his new ideas. One of the most striking results was the soundtrack for a film called *Jack Johnson*, depicting the life of the great black boxer who held the heavyweight championship of the world from 1908–15. Johnson was a controversial figure with whom Davis could readily identify, and the two long

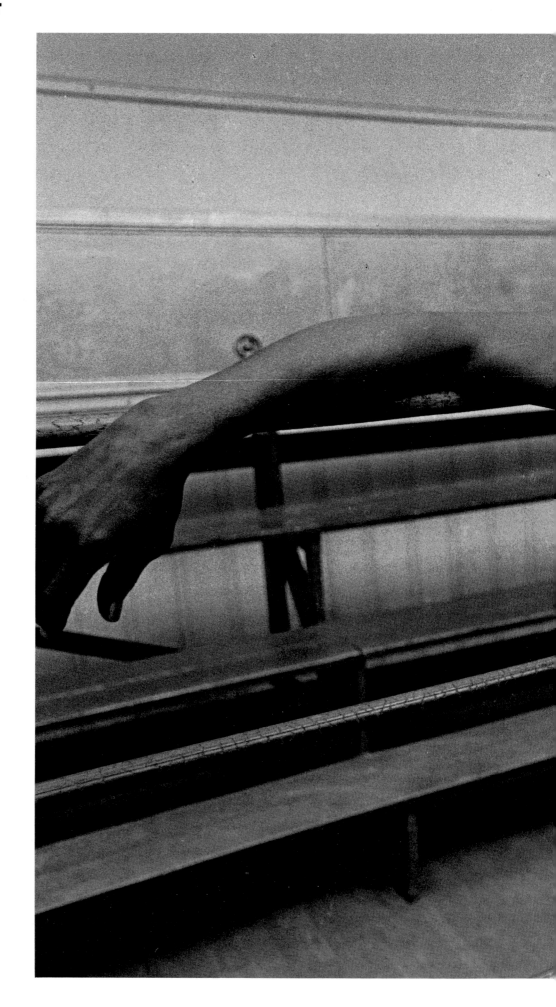

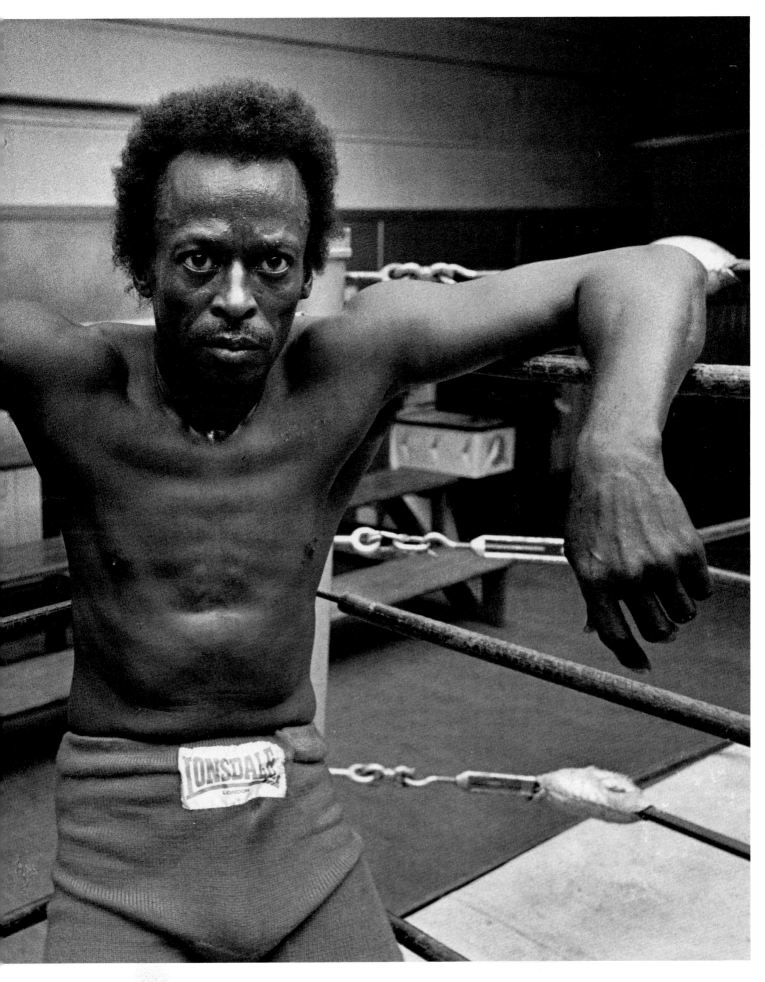

pieces making up the album displayed an aggression that cannot have been coincidental. On the piece called 'Right Off' McLaughlin played with an R&B-ish directness, while a new rhythm section – bass guitarist Michael Henderson, formerly with Stevie Wonder, and virtuoso drummer Billy Cobham – kept a powerful groove going for 20 minutes or so. This piece had all the qualities of vigour and invention that most products of the jazz-rock fusion were to lose entirely in their misguided quest for technical complexity.

On the road, Corea and the intense Jarrett, a 25-year-old from Pennsylvania with boundless confidence in his own ability, directed the band's music into more sophisticated routines, at times pushing it close to complete collective improvisation. But in its overall sound, this was probably the most unlovely band Davis ever led, thanks to the coarse timbre of the electric instruments favoured by the keyboards duo and to the uncomfortable saxophone sound of a new recruit, 19-year-old Steve Grossman from Brooklyn. Grossman and Bartz were skilled musicians, but they also represented the vanguard of a generation of stylistically anonymous saxophonists who, right up until Davis's death, failed to fill the hole left by Coltrane, Adderley, Mobley and Shorter. Albums recorded at the Fillmores revealed rather too clearly this band's unpleasantly harsh textures and improvisatory self-indulgence. Of all Davis's vast and varied recorded output, these are

Above: By 1971, the
music had become
harsher, emphasising
the abrupt rhythms
of funk. The band
now included Keith
Jarrett (piano),
Michael Henderson
(bass guitar) and
Gary Bartz (alto).

Right: Berlin, 1971:
Davis's audiences
were now divided
between the
traditionalists and
those who admired
his refusal to stand
still.

The Gemini image:
Davis backstage with
drummer Jack
DeJohnette.

At the 1971 Berlin
Jazztage, the band
appeared on the
stage of the
Philharmonic Hall.
But conventional
concert halls no
longer seemed right
for this looser, more
streetwise music.

practically the only items it is hard to imagine anyone listening to for pleasure 20, 30, 50, 100 years later.

He was, though, an even more exotically magnetic figure than ever, with a vast wardrobe of furs and leathers and an endless supply of outlandish sunglasses behind which he could practise his scowl. Around him, his former sidemen were matching him in the art of pacemaking. They had, after all, learnt from the master. Shorter and Zawinul were doing well with Weather Report, John McLaughlin's Mahavishnu Orchestra was the new sensation, Tony Williams's Lifetime was making extraordinary music, and Hancock was leading a brilliant sextet, eventually to be succeeded by the group with which he made his first dance-floor hit, 'Chameleon'. Corea and Holland, too, were partners in a remarkable outfit called Circle until the pianist went off to form his popular Brazilian-fusion outfit, Return to Forever, with Airto Moreira and his wife, the singer Flora Purim.

Davis's engagement with rock had cost him listeners, for the first time in his life. Many of those who had come to his music in the forties and fifties found themselves repelled by the volume and the weird flamboyance of his performances in the seventies. Still, he was winning polls, selling more records than ever before, playing the most prestigious events and earning a lot of money. But his life was getting no simpler. He needed an operation on troublesome hip joints. He wrecked his Lamborghini and broke his ankles when he fell asleep at speed on the West Side Highway. He'd split up with Betty. He was drinking a lot and increasing his intake of cocaine. He had trouble with nodes on his throat, and then needed treatment for a bleeding ulcer. In between all this the music was getting hotter, less European, less like recognisable jazz. In 1972, with an album called *On the Corner*, he tried to fuse the principles of Sly Stone and Karlheinz Stockhausen, producing music with a powerful and unsettling rhythmic charge. Sometimes he tried the effect of setting the serenity of Indian drums and stringed instruments against the feverish activity of his regular musicians. And releases were coming on a flood tide: *Big Fun, Live/Evil, In Concert, Get Up With It, Dark Magus, Agharta, Pangaea*. By the middle of the decade, new musicians like the guitarists Pete Cosey, Dominique Gaumont and Reggie Lucas, the drummer Al Foster and the percussionist James Mtume were helping him point the music towards darker, more introspective moods. Sometimes it churned and surged so wildly that it seemed to have passed beyond the control of the intellect.

In the summer of 1975, though, the problems became too much to bear. He was too sick, too drained, to carry on. All the drugs and all the women couldn't keep him going. He had enough money to live on. So he put his horn down and locked his front door. And for the next four years, he didn't play a note.

9

coming

back

Previous pages: **Five
years of silence
ended in 1981, with a
tour and an album.
The new direction
took Davis closer to
pop-soul music, in
collaboration with a
bunch of young
musicians as familiar
with the
Commodores as with
Coltrane.**

the missing years were filled with a
lot of the darker stuff: cocaine,
pills, booze, variety sex. Paranoid, lost,
he kept the curtains closed and the TV
on. Briefly, he went to jail for failing to
support Marguerite Eskridge, the
mother of Erin, his youngest son. Back
home, his close friends visited, but they
didn't talk. Rumours flew, but the
guesses rarely came close to the truth.
Gil Evans used to tell people that the
problem was bursitis: a drying-up of the
sacs that lubricate the elbow and knee
joints, rendering Davis incapable of
holding up the trumpet. He was playing
keyboards instead, the kindly Evans
reported. In fact he was playing nothing.

Deprived of an outlet for the creative
impulse, for the first time in his life he
began to grow nostalgic. He thought past
the moment, back into the distance of
his life. He started missing people and
things. The roll-call of the departed was
growing: Coltrane, Chambers, Kelly,
Cannonball, Mingus, Bill Evans. And,
just when the feeling was becoming
intolerable, George Butler came calling
at the brownstone on West 77th Street.

A black musicologist, Butler was now
a senior figure at Columbia Records, and
had taken it upon himself to attempt the
resuscitation of Davis's recording career.
Davis had long been publicly scornful of
what he described as his record
company's inability to market his music
to the mass of young black people as
effectively as a black-run company like
Motown. (His criticism was not entirely
justified. Although it was not a specialist
R & B label, Columbia had usually
managed to market the kind of music
young black people wanted to hear – the
fine soul singer Luther Vandross, for
instance – perfectly well.) But Butler's
warmth and erudition earned him
Davis's trust, and the gift of a new grand
piano didn't hurt. As the two men
became closer, so the possibility of a
return to activity became more likely.

Davis was roused even further from
his creative slumber by the ministrations
of the actress Cicely Tyson, whom he'd
met in the late sixties but who now began
to play a more important role in his life.
The many other women faded away as
she began to restore his health. She
introduced him to health food and
acupuncture, persuaded him to give up

Jazzhus Montmartre, Copenhagen, April 1982: in the first year of his return, Davis looked disturbingly frail, as though his fitness had disappeared during the years of silence.

Mike Stern (left), seen here at the Hammersmith Odeon in 1981, was the controversial guitarist with the comeback band, bringing an undiluted rock sensibility to the music.

smoking and got him to cut down his intake of recreational drugs.

He was attracted, too, by the idea of working with a group of Chicago musicians which included his nephew, Vincent Wilburn. He'd given Vincent his first set of drums many years earlier, and the young man had eventually graduated from the Chicago Conservatory of Music. Now, at 22, he was playing around the Chicago scene, sometimes with Davis's former guitarist, Pete Cosey, but mostly with Randy Hall, a childhood friend who played guitar and had attended the Berklee School of Music; Robert Irving III, a University of North Carolina graduate who played keyboards; and Felton Crews, a bass guitarist. All in their early 20s, they knew Davis's work, but were also fluent in the language of the Commodores and Kool and the Gang – the sort of high-technique soul music that was attracting young black musicians who, 25 years earlier, would have been imitating Art Blakey's Jazz Messengers or the Miles Davis Quintet.

Strangely enough, though, there were still such musicians, and they were playing with the Jazz Messengers. The trumpeter Wynton Marsalis and his saxophone-playing brother Branford were a pair of prodigies from New Orleans, the sons of a renowned pianist and teacher, Ellis Marsalis. Wynton, christened by Ellis in honour of Wynton Kelly, lived up to his name by mastering the most difficult period of Davis's music – the mid-sixties phase – before he

was out of his teens. At 19, in fact, he was touring European jazz festivals in a quartet with Herbie Hancock, Ron Carter and Tony Williams, sounding completely at home in the most demanding of environments. He and Branford, and other young men like the trumpeter Terence Blanchard and the altoist Donald Harrison, didn't want to play free jazz and weren't interested in soul music. Mastering post-bop music seemed like the best challenge to their technique and intellect, and they quickly became known as the 'neo-classicists'. In their suits and neat haircuts, they looked like the pictures on the back of a Blue Note sleeve, circa 1959, and they could play the music as well as its originators, if not better. Predictably, though, there was some rancour between Wynton Marsalis, the figurehead of the movement, and Davis, the man who once said, 'I have to change – it's like a curse,' and who professed disdain for young men of 19 or 20 who couldn't find a music of their own to play. His irritation was certainly compounded by the fact that Columbia, his own label, was putting a major commercial push behind Marsalis's first solo album – an effort that he felt could well have been applied to his own products.

Anyone who hoped that the return of Miles Davis meant a reactivation of 'My Funny Valentine' was going to be disappointed. Davis was much more interested in what he had in common with young men like Wilburn, Hall, Irving and Crews, whom he first heard

Corporate loyalty: when Columbia gave a party to celebrate his return, Davis reciprocated by wearing a Willie Nelson baseball cap.

157

on tape during a phone conversation with his sister Dorothy in 1980. He called them to New York, and they began recording together. This, he soon decided, was the new direction, the sound with which he could relaunch himself. 'There's something for everybody,' Randy Hall told *Down Beat*, trying to describe it. 'Vocals, electronics, to appeal to young people. It's commercial enough that people who never heard Miles before will get it. Older fans of his will dig it, too. Some tunes are, like, pop.'

The Man with the Horn was the album's title, and it lived up to Hall's description. There was more of a sense of song-form than in the work of the 1970–75 bands, without the endless jamming. The title track, a glutinous soul ballad sung by Hall, seemed out of place on a

record by the man who once directed *Kind of Blue*, but most of the music had a spirited tautness. A new young saxophonist, the confusingly named Bill Evans, sounded up to the post-Shorter standard, and the trumpet-playing was fine.

It wasn't always so fine on his comeback tour, though, when his physical frailty stood exposed. Davis's importance had never been based on his technical prowess; indeed, it was often said that his mistakes were more valuable than most other trumpeters' clean hits. But no one was quite prepared for the thin, stooped, hobbling figure who drew up outside a Boston club in the spring of 1981 in a brand new yellow Ferrari. For four nights in Boston and then at Avery Fisher Hall in New York as part of the Newport Jazz Festival, Davis presented his new band before setting off for Japan and Europe. Some of the tunes were those premièred on the comeback album, but the music had largely reverted to the more relaxed pacing of the early seventies, partly through the return of Al Foster, the experienced drummer who could inject the spontaneity of bebop into the rhythmic patterns of funk. Bill Evans, a 23-year-old from Chicago, was there, with a young guitarist, Mike Stern, who had played with Billy Cobham's band and a late edition of Blood Sweat & Tears. The percussionist, Mino Cinelu, had a father from Martinique, grew up in Paris and was spotted by Davis playing with a soul band at a New York club.

During the early eighties, Davis became more and more keen on painting. Eventually a book of his artworks was published.

The most important member of the band, though, was the bass guitarist. Marcus Miller, introduced to Davis by Bill Evans, knew jazz inside out, but was also completely comfortable with soul music. Among his credits was an important role in Luther Vandross's first hit album in 1981, a work of outstanding musicianship. Miller played further down his instrument's register than most bass guitarists, giving the music – whether Vandross's or Davis's – a deep, lush carpet; his grasp of structure and texture also made him an outstanding arranger, composer and producer, a combination of talents which was to make him vitally important to his new employer.

If Miller's value was immediately apparent, Mike Stern's was far less obvious to most people. Stern drew from his Fender Broadcaster a heavily treated sound that many critics felt belonged on a rock record; looking for a way to disparage the music without criticising the obviously convalescent Davis, they picked on Stern. They were wrong. *We Want Miles*, the live album recorded during that summer's concerts, revealed a careful, sensitive and spirited player whose contribution to a 20-minute version of 'My Man's Gone Now' was as integral to the success of one of Davis's greatest latter-day recordings as the superlative playing of Miller and Foster.

Davis played mostly from a chair during that 1981 tour; many of his trumpet notes came out cracked and split. When he put a long blues phrase together, the poignancy was rendered almost unbearable by the knowledge of the effort it was costing him. By the time he returned to Europe in the summer of 1982, though, he seemed rehabilitated. Now married to Cicely Tyson (on Thanksgiving Day 1981, at Bill Cosby's house, with Andrew Young as minister and Max Roach as best man), he sat in a London hotel room with a dozen felt-tip pens and an A2 sketch pad, drawing exotic female figures that took the mind back to Mati Klarwein's strange, compelling painting on the cover of *Bitches Brew* a dozen years earlier. He talked with equal interest about the past and the present, about J.J. Johnson and Michael Jackson, about trumpet tone and synthesiser programmes. He talked about the herbs that his Chinese doctor was giving him, and about the value of swimming for breath control. He mentioned that he had to wear a truss, but was keen to show how hard and strong his stomach muscles had become. He was alert, combative and amusing; and the next night, at Hammersmith Odeon, he played with something approaching his old fire.

Star People, the album recorded that year, introduced a new guitarist, John Scofield, alongside Stern. The title track, an 18-minute blues, found Davis reaching back to the music he must have heard in childhood for a performance of affecting simplicity. Some of his drawings, in acid greens and oranges, adorned the sleeve. The pressure was raised the following year with *Decoy*,

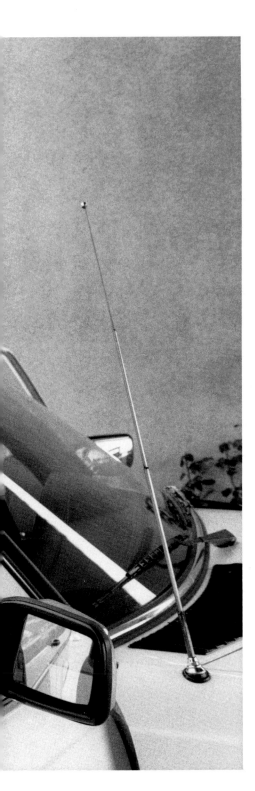

The saxophonist Bob Berg joined Davis at the suggestion of his predecessor, Bill Evans, and stayed three years. This is Wembley Conference Centre, November 1984.

At the jazz festival in Nîmes, southern France, in the summer of 1984. Illness was beginning to cost him his hair.

His last years were studded with honours. In December 1984, in Copenhagen, he received the Leonie Sonning Award for a lifetime's achievement in music.

Never a candidate for the nostalgia circuit, he sprinkled his new repertoire with items borrowed from Michael Jackson, Cyndi Lauper and the British avant-pop group Scritti Politti.

another studio album on which Foster, Cinelu, Scofield and Irving were joined by a powerful new bass guitarist, Darryl Jones, and Branford Marsalis. Jones's hard attack added an urgency that fitted well with what Scofield and Irving were up to: the music lost the flowing quality that Stern and Miller had brought, and started sounding like something you might hear on the radio in mid-1984: sharp, slick, contemporary, with a less central role for improvisation. *You're Under Arrest*, the following year, took the process even further: on the cover, the black-clad Davis – black stetson, black embroidered jacket, black leather trousers – cradled an automatic weapon. On the first track, his trademark croak recited a story about being stopped by the California police while driving the yellow Ferrari near the new beach house he and Cicely had built in Malibu. But the pieces that attracted most attention were versions of two recent pop hits, Michael Jackson's 'Human Nature' and Cyndi Lauper's 'Time After Time'. Simple, winsome tunes, they were given Davis's best tight-muted treatment over Irving's warm synthesiser washes. What's the difference, Davis was saying, between me playing 'The Surrey With a Fringe on Top' or 'Bye Bye Blackbird' in 1955 and these tunes in 1985? His answer: none. Same player, same instincts. If you couldn't keep up, too bad.

There were still plenty of people who would rather have been listening to 'Bye Bye Blackbird', but by now they'd

abandoned hope. Nevertheless, Davis was being offered the gold watches for a long and illustrious career. And, interestingly, he wasn't turning them down. In 1983 Columbia had hosted a tribute concert at Radio City Music Hall, during which he had received an honorary degree from Fisk University. Quincy Jones, Herbie Hancock, George Benson, Jackie McLean, Tony Williams and others had been present to pay their respects. And in 1984 he went to Denmark to receive the Sonning Award, presented for a lifetime achievement in music. Three months later he returned to take part in the recording of a suite the organisers had commissioned in his honour from one of his most talented European disciples, the Danish trumpeter and composer Palle Mikkelborg. The hour-long *Aura*, as Mikkelborg titled it, ranged over the whole gamut of Davis's career, paying homage without descending into pastiche. The 30-piece orchestra included electronic keyboards, double bass and bass guitar, brass and reeds, a harp, a female voice and John McLaughlin's guitar. Impressed by Mikkelborg's skill and sensitivity, Davis was inspired to some of the most concentrated work of his later years, although it took Columbia four years to get around to releasing it.

The reason was his departure from the label, which took place after the release of *You're Under Arrest* and ended a turbulent 30-year relationship which had produced an extraordinary amount of

The Danish trumpeter Palle Mikkelborg composed a remarkable suite, titled *Aura*, in Davis's honour, and in February 1985 they recorded the work in Copenhagen. *Right:* in the studio with the guitarist John McLaughlin. *Left:* with McLaughlin's companion, the classical pianist Katia Labèque. *Below:* with Mikkelborg.

Below: **On stage in Copenhagen, October 1985, showing the trumpet microphone that allowed him to move around the stage as freely as a guitarist.**

Left: **His own playing had good nights and bad ones in the eighties, but there was always enough to tell you that this was Miles Davis.**

Festival Hall, London, July 1985: Darryl Jones had replaced Marcus Miller on bass, bringing a new edge to the rhythms.

great music. Albums like *Kind of Blue* and *Sketches of Spain* would stay in print around the world; the tins of unreleased live and studio material could be plundered for valuable archive projects in years to come.

Davis's eyes, as ever, were on the future. 'I don't play that way no more' was his standard response to those who asked him to revisit former glories, and to inaugurate his new recording contract with Warner Brothers he planned something different. He called Marcus Miller, whose career as a producer had been gathering pace, and asked him to listen to some music he'd been sent by the keyboards player George Duke. Miller had been talking to Tommy LiPuma, the Warners producer responsible for the company's new acquisition. Miller went into his own eight-track studio, worked on a couple of tunes, overdubbing all the parts himself, and flew to California to play the demos to Davis and LiPuma. The demos turned out to be the basis for the album, with Miller playing keyboards, bass, percussion, soprano saxophone and bass clarinet. Other musicians were brought in here and there – drummer Omar Hakim on one track, percussionist Paulinho Da Costa on another, violinist Michal Urbaniak on a third. George Duke played most of the instruments on his own composition, but Miller was the true architect and the builder of the album that became known as *Tutu*, in a dedication to the South African civil rights leader and Nobel laureate.

With *Tutu*, Davis entered another world. This was music beyond category. Who cared what had been improvised in real time, or what had been sliced together at the editing table? Who cared whether the strings were real wood-and-gut violins, or a programme stored in a micro-chip? There was a place for the old ways, but since it was impossible to uninvent the computer, you had to deal with the consequences. *Tutu* was a record of outstanding beauty, and there was no shame in the fact that it could sound as much at home as a background to the hubbub of a busy coffee house as on an expensive domestic stereo system. What was wrong with that? Miles Davis

Copenhagen, 1985: Davis relished the interplay with his enthusiastic young sidemen, but sometimes the old solitary spirit would break through.

London, 1985: now there were two guitarists. Jazz purists found the contributions of John Scofield (left) more palatable than those of Mike Stern.

never thought that music should be above functionality. (And he answered the criticism that the tunes on *Tutu* were no better than soundtrack music for *Miami Vice* in the wittiest way: in 1986, at the height of the TV series's popularity, he made a guest appearance, playing a dope-dealing pimp in the most self-ironising screen cameo since the pop record producer Phil Spector played a coke dealer in the opening sequence of *Easy Rider* in 1969.)

As a sort of follow-up to 'Human Nature' and 'Time After Time', *Tutu* contained a version of a song called 'Perfect Way', by the English pop group Scritti Politti, who returned the compliment by inviting Davis to make a guest appearance on one of their own records, 'Oh Patti', a hit in 1988. He was also getting involved with Prince, the most creative figure in soul music at the end of the eighties. The natural successor to James Brown, Sly Stone and Stevie Wonder as the music's moving force, Prince invited Davis to his Minneapolis headquarters, where they worked briefly but unconclusively together.

Gil Evans, the collaborator with whom Davis had enjoyed the longest and most fruitful relationship, died in

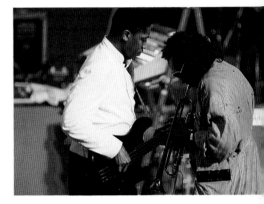

Copenhagen, 1987: Davis took particular delight in the extrovert playing of another new bass guitarist, Foley McCreary.

Right: He'd begun playing electronic keyboards during the seventies, when he was too weak to hold up the trumpet for long periods. Now it became integral to his activities, although he usually restricted himself to holding chords in the background of the music.

Left: London, 1986, with Bob Berg: as the music got louder, so did the wardrobe.

Opposite: **Festival Hall, London, 1989: a hair-weave was disguising his encroaching baldness, caused by treatment for his illnesses.**

Below: **Married to the actress Cicely Tyson in the mid-eighties, he built a new home in Malibu, by the Pacific ocean.**

Mexico in March 1988 after a long illness. Two months before his death, he had called Davis to talk about a project they'd discussed many years earlier: a version of Puccini's *Tosca*. But Evans was a slow worker, and it would probably never have happened. 'Gil was my best friend,' Davis later said, 'but he never was together in terms of being organised.' That looseness, though, was Evans's gift to Davis and to the world: it was the temperament that allowed him to glimpse the virtue of slowing the music down, of stripping away the harmonic undergrowth, of letting people see the beauty of Miles Davis's sound. 'To me,' Davis added, 'Gil is not dead.'

Marcus Miller returned for Davis's next studio album, the soundtrack to an Anglo-American feature film called *Siesta*, starring Ellen Barkin and Gabriel Byrne. Miller wrote the music, and took joint billing with Davis on the sleeve; tucked away in the corner were these words: 'This album is dedicated to Gil Evans, The Master.' Taking the film's Spanish setting, Miller had constructed a suite of tone poems which evoked *Sketches of Spain*, paid homage to it and went beyond it to create an autonomous work using the materials of its own era. Again Miller played almost everything, with the assistance of his synthesiser programmer Jason Miles. Some of the pieces were fragments; others were fully conceived. They drew from Davis his best and truest playing in years, some of it compressed into isolated and cryptic phrases that hung and glowed in the air. As with *Tutu*, the artificial nature of the music's construction was completely beside the point. All that mattered was how the end result sounded. *Siesta* made a perfect circle with the soundtrack to *Ascenseur pour l'échafaud*, 31 years earlier. The film itself turned out to be negligible, and was forgotten within weeks of its brief appearance in the cinemas, but the album deserved a prominent position among Davis's output.

The third Davis/Miller collaboration came out a year later. *Amandla* continued where *Tutu* had left off, although it made more use of other musicians – Al Foster, the guitarist Jean-Paul Bourelly, the pianist Joe Sample

Left & below: By the late eighties he was touring almost as obsessively as Bob Dylan. Here he is at the Hague (*top*).

and a new saxophonist, Kenny Garrett, who was now a regular member of Davis's touring band.

By this time, many more musicians had come and gone through the ranks. No longer, though, was membership of the Davis entourage an automatic passport to stardom as a soloist. The saxophonists Steve Grossman, Dave Liebman, Gary Bartz, Bill Evans and Bob Berg, keyboardists Robert Irving, Adam Holzman and Kei Akagi, bassists Foley McCreary and Benjamin Rietveld, drummers and percussionists Ricky Wellman, Marilyn Mazur, Steve Thornton and Rudy Bird – these were not destined to follow Adderley, Coltrane, Garland, Shorter, Hancock, Carter, Williams and the pianist Bill Evans into the ranks of the immortals.

Amandla had one surprise: a piece called 'Mr Pastorius', dedicated to the murdered virtuoso bass guitarist Jaco Pastorius, who had made his reputation alongside Joe Zawinul and Wayne Shorter in Weather Report during the seventies. Here Miller created a piece based on the precepts laid down for *Miles Ahead*. His soloist responded with a perfect recreation of the tender lyricism of the late fifties. 'I don't play that way no more'? Now he did, and the sound of it was almost unbearably moving.

As, in a very different way, was his appearance on another soundtrack album the following year. For Dennis Hopper's thriller *The Hot Spot*, composer/producer Jack Nitzsche put together one

of the strangest combinations imaginable, juxtaposing the 64-year-old Davis, the ultimate sophisticate, with the 73-year-old John Lee Hooker, the guitarist and singer from Clarksdale, Mississippi, whose playing was perhaps closer to the African roots than that of any other living bluesman. What did they have in common? Plenty, as it turned out. The common root was enough, and the album contained moments in which two kinds of dark, hypnotic power combined to form a third. In the track called 'Murder', based on one of Hooker's oldest one-chord riffs, as Davis spat out his muted epigrams over Hooker's sinister humming, they seemed to be getting to the heart of something important, whatever it was.

Peering into the front stalls at Hammersmith Odeon, July 1990.

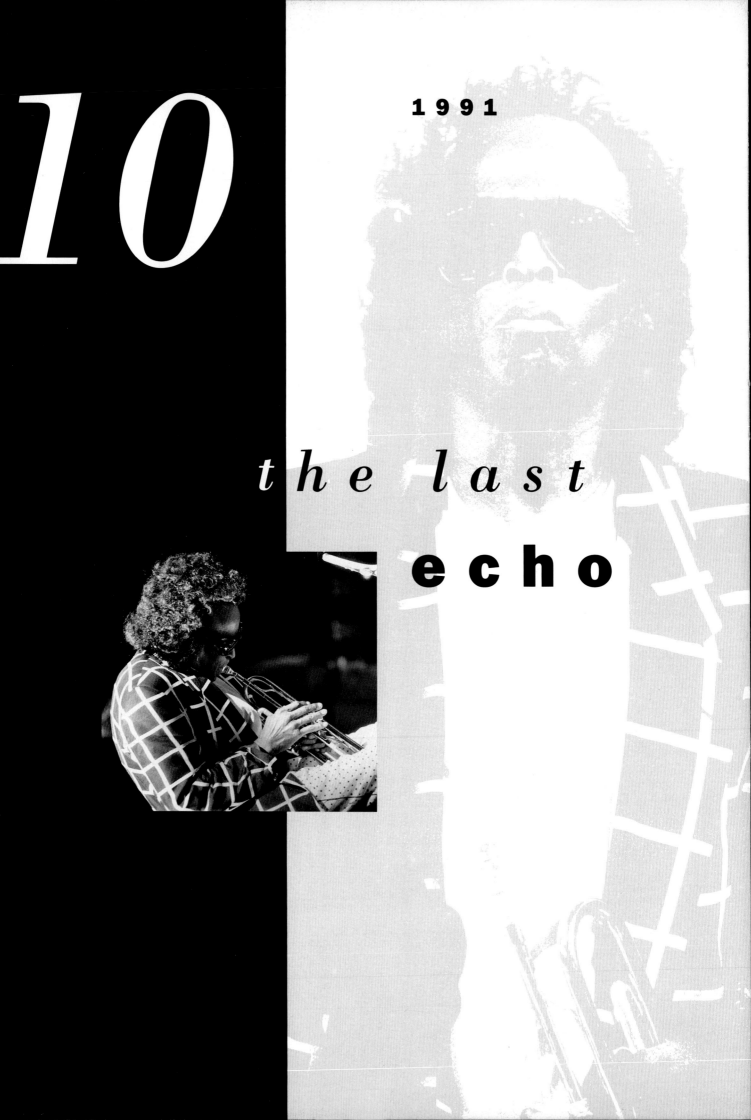

10

1991

the last

echo

Don't look back.

Never apologise, never
explain.

Say something once, why say it
again?

these were the maxims by which
Miles Davis lived, so it was a real
surprise when he published his
autobiography in 1989. Written in
collaboration with a journalist, Quincy

**Previous page: On
8 July 1991, in the
lakeside town of
Montreux, Miles
Davis played the
arrangements of his
old friend Gil Evans
for the first time in
30 years. Shocked by
his apparent frailty,
the audience was
soon amazed by his
devotion to the task
of recreating the
classics of his past.**

Troupe, it was immediately notable for
its vivid transcription of the subject's
spoken thoughts. Its true value, though,
was in the quality of Davis's recollection
and judgement. He turned out to have
forgotten nothing, and to have
remembered why he'd done it, and how
it all felt. Unsparing of himself and
others, it was nevertheless generous and
affectionate towards those he admired.
What it didn't attempt was to resolve the
contradictions of his life. Life, he was
telling us, is full of contradictions; that's
how it is.

On one of his last European tours he
gave the *Herald Tribune*'s Mike Zwerin,
who had briefly played trombone with
the great nonet at the Royal Roost in
1948, his best explanation of his refusal
to look over his shoulder: 'We play what
the day recommends.' It is matched only
by the architect Frank Gehry's
justification of his extreme modernism:
if I simply repeated the past, Gehry said,
how would I explain to my children that
I couldn't respond to my own times?
Now Davis was listening to rap and hip-
hop, the next phase in the evolution of
Afro-American vernacular music. He
called Russell Simmons, the head of Def
Jam Records, a leading rap label, to help
him find new people to work with.
Simmons led him to a rapper called Easy
Moe Bee. Later, an album was released:
Doo-Bop was full of funny little raps,
tight trumpet, slack rhythms and slick
samples from Kool and the Gang and
Young-Holt Unlimited.

But on 8 July 1991 Miles Davis gave

Left: On the last dates with his own band, the music maintained its ferocity and its insistence on confronting its own times.

Below: The Montreux concert was the fruit of long persuasion by Quincy Jones, who spanned almost the same number of musical eras as Davis, and took the baton to conduct the 50-piece orchestra.

us the biggest surprise of all. At the Palais des Festivals in Montreux, by the shore of Lac Léman, he turned up to revisit his past. Fronting 50 musicians from America and Europe, under the baton of his old friend Quincy Jones, he played the music written for him by Gil Evans. It was something we never thought we'd see.

The first shock, at the afternoon rehearsal, was that we – those of us who'd talked our way past the security –

knew the music better than he did. As he groped through the complex opening fanfares of 'The Pan Piper', from *Sketches of Spain*, as the notes cracked and flew off beyond the control of his spindly fingers, you couldn't help realising that while you'd held this music next to your heart for 30 years, gradually committing its every detail to memory, he hadn't. He had played it once, and moved on.

Of all the century's great artists,

In Paris on 10 July 1991, Davis was invested as a Commander of Arts and Letters by the Minister of Culture, and celebrated with a concert featuring old colleagues, among them Wayne Shorter (left) and Dave Holland (centre).

perhaps only Picasso was as hooked as Miles Davis on the dynamic of change, on the high of leading from the front. What this meant was that if you weren't around when *Kind of Blue* or *Porgy and Bess* were made, that was your bad luck. It was real-time music. And eventually it became possible to accept his decision. After all, it wasn't really Davis's attitude that was so amazing; it was the fact that so many other musicians were prepared to spend the rest of their lives repeating themselves.

'I've been wanting Miles to do this for 15 years,' Quincy Jones said. 'I kept talking to him about it, and I guess I wore him down.' But Miles Davis wasn't someone you could wear down. He must have had his reasons. He wasn't up for explanations – 'Would you leave me be?' he rasped, when interrupted while reading his sheet music in the stalls – but what the project meant to him was evident from the ferocious concentration glinting in his liquid brown eyes.

He had passed 65 in May. A life of excess had brought him 20 years of gathering infirmity. But he guarded his masculinity like a shield, so it was touching to hear that he had requested the presence of a second trumpeter, the gifted young Wallace Roney, to share the soloist's role. What this meant to Davis could only be imagined, particularly since the handsome, well-built Roney looked not unlike the Davis of 40 years earlier, when he was making his reputation.

Roney helped out on the high-note

With Foley McCreary at the Festival Hall on 19 July 1991, on his last visit to London.

sections of 'Springsville' and 'Blues for Pablo', and took several solos, but Davis was far from total abdication, and played on 'Boplicity', 'Maids of Cadiz' and 'My Ship' with the freshness of a boy and the control of a mature man. After each piece, the applause was held for minutes, as if no one wanted to let the music go.

Left & below: In Paris, with the saxophonist Bill Evans and with Holland and Shorter. Davis's paintings formed the backdrops.

Below: **Sound-check in Paris with Joe Zawinul (in cap, left) and John McLaughlin (right).**

Left: **Paris had been where he found himself as a man and a musician during his visits in 1949 and 1957. Now it was a station on what turned out to be his farewell tour.**

Right: London, 1991.

Finally, unforgettably, on trooped the bassoons, the oboes, the flutes and the harp, augmenting the orchestra for two pieces from *Sketches of Spain*. In 'Solea', the implacable snare-drum tattoo gathered intensity while waves of brass came echoing as if from the walls of ancient Andalusian streets. Davis's shouts pierced the mass with heart-stopping cries: the deepest of deep songs.

You couldn't help wondering what he was up to. Physically, he looked extraordinary. He was obviously frail,

Below: Montreux, 1991.

Right: London, 1991.

his wrists as thin as a girl's, and he was having trouble getting up even the shallow steps to the stage. Under the extravagant wig that hid the baldness which afflicted him in the early eighties, and which his vanity would not let him show, his face was fine, delicate, beautiful, ageless and unutterably fierce. His wardrobe was as extravagant as ever: fine silks in wild colours. For as long as he was in the room, he was the focal point. When he played, musicians as experienced as the trumpeter Lew Soloff, the saxophonist George Adams and the drummer Grady Tate watched him as if it were for the last time.

Wallace Roney talked later about the conversations they'd had. 'He was telling me everything he could think of about music, like he was trying to cram 45 years of music into three days.'

A couple of days later he was at it again. In Paris, he received a decoration from the Minister of Culture and played another celebratory concert, this time with a small group. Herbie Hancock, Wayne Shorter and Jackie McLean were among those who took the stage to play a fond set with him. The meaning of all this was becoming clear.

His last show was at the Hollywood Bowl six weeks later. Wayne Shorter went to see him. 'I noticed he was much more fragile than in Paris,' Shorter was to say. 'The last number that he played, I knew he was tired. It was the first time I ever heard that kind of fatigue coming from him. Now I know, it was the illness.'

Early in September, there were sudden rumours that he was in hospital, in a coma. Reassuring counter-statements were issued. But on Saturday 29 September 1991, at St John's Hospital and Health Center in Santa Monica, just down the coast from his Malibu home, he died. His doctor, Jeff Harris, announced the cause as pneumonia, respiratory failure and a stroke.

The grieving around the world was immediate and intense. The guitarist Pat Metheny voiced a common thought when he said it felt as though the music had stopped, that without Davis's presence in the world, further progress seemed impossible. 'Miles was a resonance,' Keith Jarrett remarked. 'And when he died, we lost the resonance.' But it was more than just the loss of a great musician, a great artist. It was the removal of a symbol of independence of thought and action, whether we had been inspired to achieve it too or, more likely, had fallen back and failed.

He could be brusque, blunt, cruel. But here's what Juliette Gréco thought of him. 'I never thought about him being black,' she told *Libération*. 'To me, he was simply beautiful. And he was always very *gentil*. Three or four years ago, he came to see me. He was sitting over there, and at one point I got up and turned my back. And I heard him laugh. "Why are you laughing?" I asked. He replied: "That back, that way of moving, I believe I'll remember them wherever I am in the world." '

**The man, the green
shirt, 1958.**

a c k n o w l e d g e m e n t s

The following books were consulted in the preparation of this manuscript:

Miles: The Autobiography, Miles Davis with Quincy Troupe (Simon & Schuster/Macmillan, 1989).

Miles Davis: A Critical Biography, Ian Carr (Quartet, 1982).

Miles Davis: A Musical Biography, Bill Cole (William Morrow, 1974).

Bird Lives, Ross Russell (Quartet, 1973).

To Be Or Not To Bop: The Autobiography of Dizzy Gillespie, with Al Fraser (W. H. Allen, 1980).

Material has been drawn from the author's conversations with Gil Evans, Max Roach, John Lewis, Gerry Mulligan, Herbie Hancock, Tony Williams, Wayne Shorter, Dave Holland, Keith Jarrett and John McLaughlin.

The author wishes to record his thanks to the following writers: Val Wilmer, Michael Zwerin, Martin Williams, Max Harrison, André Hodeir, Charles Fox, Nat Hentoff, Don DeMichael, Ralph Gleason, John Fordham, Michael Cuscuna, Ira Gitler, Amiri Baraka (LeRoi Jones), Joachim-Ernst Berendt, Whitney Balliett, Brian Case, Kenneth Tynan, Gary Giddins, Pete Welding, Max Jones, Alun Morgan, Leonard Feather, John A. Tynan, Bob Blumenthal, David Wild and Brian Priestley.

With thanks to Nesuhi Ertegun and Robert Fripp; and to Tim de Lisle for the title.

index